A DEVIL'S CALDRON

The thermals spread out four miles laterally from the center of the fire. Japanese fighter pilots in the air over Tokyo reported they were unable to control their light airplanes, that they were flung helplessly around the sky and could not swing into pursuit curves to attack the racing B-29's.

B-29's at six thousand feet were caught by the shattering force of the superheated air, and flipped upside down, onto their backs. Often the planes fell several thousand feet before the shaken pilots could recover.

One bomber was caught in a particularly severe rising column of superheated air. Without warning the heavy airplane shot skyward, the pilot helpless at the controls. Within several seconds the airplane was flung from seven thousand to more than twelve thousand feet; the nose flashed upward, went straight up, and in those few seconds the B-29 was inverted at nearly two and a half miles above the city. By some miracle, the Superfortress completed its maneuver with the crew and all loose gear against the ceiling, fell down and back in a screaming loop, and streaked earthward. With both the pilot and co-pilot straining with all their might the airplane came out of its wild plunge only two hundred feet over Tokyo Bay. Wings bent sharply upward from the terrible strain, the B-29 leveled out at nearly 450 miles per hour and went howling out of range of the shore guns before the astonished Japanese could react.

THE BANTAM WAR BOOK SERIES

This series of books is about a world on fire.

The carefully chosen volumes in the Bantam War Book Series cover the full dramatic sweep of World War II. Many are eyewitness accounts by the men who fought in a global conflict as the world's future hung in the balance. Fighter pilots, tank commanders and infantry captains, among many others, recount exploits of individual courage. They present vivid portraits of brave men, true stories of gallantry, moving sagas of survival and stark tragedies of untimely death.

In 1933 Nazi Germany marched to become an empire that was to last a thousand years. In only twelve years that empire was destroyed, and the country was bisected by her conquerors. Italy relinquished her colonial lands, as did Japan. These were the losers. The winners also lost the empires they had so painfully seized over the centuries. And one, Russia, lost over twenty million dead.

Those wartime 1940s were a simple, even a hopeful time. Hats came in only two colors, white and black, and after an initial battering the Allied nations started on a long laborious march toward victory. It was a time when sane men believed the world would evolve into a decent place, but, as with all futures, there was no one then who could really forecast the world that we know now.

There are many ways to think about war. It has always been hard to understand the motivations and braveries of Axis soldiers fighting to enslave and dominate their neighbors. Yet it is impossible to know the hammer without the anvil, and to comprehend ourselves we must know the people we once fought against.

Through these books we can discover what it was like to take part in the war that was a final experience for nearly fifty million human beings. In so doing we may discover the strength to make a world as good as the one contained in those dreams and aspirations once believed by heroic men. We must understand our past as an honor to those dead who can no longer choose. They exchanged their lives in a hope for this future that we now inhabit. Though the fight took place many years ago, each of us remains as a living part of it.

A TORCH TO THE ENEMY

The Fire Raid on Tokyo

MARTIN CAIDIN

BANTAM BOOKS
NEW YORK • TORONTO • LONDON • SYDNEY • AUCKLAND

This edition contains the complete text
of the original hardcover edition.
NOT ONE WORD HAS BEEN OMITTED.

A TORCH TO THE ENEMY

A Bantam Falcon Book / published by arrangement with
the author

PUBLISHING HISTORY

Bantam edition / November 1992

ISBN 0-553-29926-3

Published simultaneously in the United States and Canada

PRINTED IN THE UNITED STATES OF AMERICA

OPM   0 9 8 7 6 5 4 3 2 1

CONTENTS

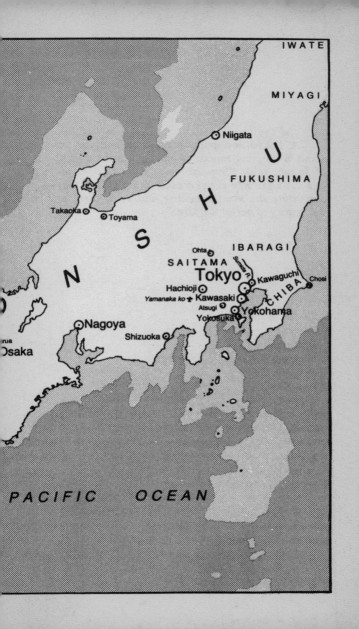

A Tokyo newspaperman, when interviewed about B-29 crew reports of damage to the capital of Japan, said: *"Superfortress reports of damage . . . were not exaggerated: if anything, they constitute the most shocking understatement in the history of aerial warfare."*

PREFACE

Exactly at noon of March 10th, 1945, Imperial Japanese Headquarters in the city of Tokyo, on the main Japanese island of Honshu, released the following communiqué:

"From a little past midnight to 0240 hours today, March 10th, about one hundred and thirty B-29 bombers attacked Tokyo with the mainstay of their strength, and carried out indiscriminate bombings of the city area.

"The indiscriminate bombings caused fires at various places in the capital. The fire at Shumeryo [headquarters building] of the Imperial Household Ministry was put under control at 0235 and others not later than 0800.

"War results thus far verified include fifteen planes shot down and fifty others damaged."

Fred Saito, former news broadcaster and commentator for Radio Tokyo during World War II, and today a crack newspaper reporter for Associated Press in Japan, waved a yellowed copy of the original communiqué which had been broadcast from his Tokyo studios back in 1945. We had just completed a search through voluminous official files on what was the most devastating air attack suffered by Japan during World War II. It was a savage air raid in which the combination of people killed, maimed, and missing, plus the great area destroyed by a raging holocaust, made it the single most effective aerial assault of the entire war. Fred Saito personally spent several months walking the streets of Tokyo, the city he knew better than any other, tracking down survivors of the worst of that fire.

Fred knew this raid well—he was in Tokyo, but fortunately away from the center of the attack—when the bombers struck.

He waved the communiqué. "It is really hard," he said, "to discover another statement that could be so hypocritical. You do a lot of things in wartime that just aren't done on other occasions, but in all my memory—and in all the archives we've gone through—this is really it.

"Certain things are immediately obvious to us, of course, because we know what really happened. And if you know how to read between the lines. . . . "

Significant in the communiqué—significant to the Japanese who knew at the time what really had happened—however, was the omission of the cliché that always marked every previous statement issued after a raid, insisting vehemently that the damage sustained in the attacked Japanese city was "negligible."

"Our newspapers in those days," Fred continued, "were all controlled tightly by the military censors. There wasn't any questioning of that rule, or the editor was liable to find his head rolling on the ground. The papers simply weren't allowed to contradict anything that came out of Imperial Headquarters. But on March 11th—and this caused a lot of eyebrows to go up—the papers all carried a little more than they were allowed to say. It wasn't much, but believe me, it amounted to an editorial revolt against our war leaders."

I spoke to several of these newspaper editors, and they all recalled those moments when the shock of the aftereffects of the raid drove them to what was, in the face of rigid government control, sheer recklessness. In all previous air attacks, the papers reported only what was contained in the communiqués handed down to them. This time, however, they pinpointed exactly the sites where three of the large American bombers crashed: at Itabashi Village of Ibaragi Prefecture, Fukuda Village of Chiba Prefecture, and in the suburbs of Kawaguchi City.

This was a direct affront to the military, which in its communiqué stated that fifteen bombers were "shot down and fifty others damaged." The reports made it clear that these three wrecks were the only known ones resulting from Japanese defenses, and constituted indirect scorn of the military claims.

It is difficult, if not altogether impossible, for the Westerner to appreciate the magnitude of such steps. Japan was a country in which all public forms of communication had been rigidly controlled for many years. The Japanese nation endured a "thought police" organization the like of which not even Germany with her Gestapo and SS ever knew. Any Japanese citizen—or editor, or broadcaster— could be accused of indulging in "dangerous thoughts," dragged out of his home in the middle of the night and shot at once.

Under such conditions, intellectual revolt is hardly a recommended occupation. The Japanese editors later were shocked at their own audacity. But there was good reason for that revolt—in the stench of burning flesh that permeated the air of the city, in the great scar that had been ripped in the heart of downtown Tokyo, in the dazed and horrified eyes of those human beings, burned viciously, who had staggered away from the fire area.

Upon reflection, the editors were even more amazed at the sudden timidity of the military censors who ruled their lives and passed sentence upon their every word. Apparently even these stolid people had been shaken, for they found themselves unable to maintain their air of aloof superiority before the editors who, obviously enraged, came to their offices to have their copy censored. The newspaper *Asahi*, in an editorial cleared by these censors, stated in part:

" . . . our capital suffered from damage on an unprecedented scale . . . an air raid of this terrible sort could well have been prepared for. We cannot deny the fact that our side was completely unprepared and unforgivably ill-equipped for such a contingency. We must give the most serious reflection. . . . "

Although worded with painstaking care, the editorial was read by the Japanese public as an unprecedented admission of the fantastic damage wrought by the American bombers. That the newspaper would print what amounted to a flat contradiction of an official statement from Impe-

rial Headquarters constituted the first breach that the people
had ever known in the rigid security system; more important, what was left unsaid, what could be read between the
lines, made these people ponder deeply the true course of
the war.

Never until this moment in the course of Japan's travels along her road of military conquest had the nation's
newspapers resorted to outright criticism of the military.
This was almost as earth-shaking as the aerial attack itself,
for the Japanese are quick to find meaning where it is
barely hinted, and in Japanese terms the chiding of the military was equivalent—in the United States—to screaming
headlines and bitter invective. What prompted people to depart from their accustomed acquiescence to government
propaganda was the clear inference that the war was going
not at all well, and that the horror so recently inflicted upon
the "sacred soil of Japan" (which the military leaders had
shouted would never know the impact of an enemy bomb)
might be the forerunner of even greater savagery in fire.

For the first time a deep undercurrent of fear ran
through Japan. This is not to say, that until this moment the
Japanese had disregarded the intense attacks mounting
daily upon their cities and factories. But the majority of
such attacks were with high-explosive bombs. Their weight
was concentrated primarily upon industrial targets and the
cities had been spared the holocausts which every Japanese
learns to fear almost from childhood.

The reader must understand the basic difference between the stoic Japanese acceptance of disaster and the way
such events are regarded in our own land by our own people. With so many millions of human beings thrust into a
comparatively small geographical area, the Japanese know
intimately the sufferings of their neighbors. Moreover, they
live in a land where disaster is commonplace, where catastrophe is only a matter of time, where death may strike in
a terrible sweep through great areas.

This is the history of Japan and its people; a grim history of terrible earthquakes, of roaring tidal waves, of
avalanches and floods. Every Japanese city by the very nature of its flimsy, wooden structures has always been a potential firetrap; thickly populated, weak on water supply

and fire-fighting equipment, the cities have often been gutted by unquenchable flames.

Thus the initial B-29 attacks were little more than disaster delivered through a new medium—the enemy and his bombs. But it was so unique a means of delivery, it was so unprecedented, that police measures were used in the most severe fashion to restrict any details of the bombings. The Japanese accepted their bombings, tightened their belts, and continued their faith in their country and in ultimate victory.

But now . . . the hell wrought in Tokyo could not simply be eliminated or forgotten by refusal to face the horror of the greatest number of dead ever resulting from a single sweep of flame. Rumors spread and fear was nourished in the haggard eyes of the survivors. Travel into Tokyo was restricted, for a single look at the ash-choked wasteland was enough to strike the lie to the insistent claims of "negligible damage."

The censors of Japan moved cautiously, and raised the curtain on the news of the bombing; it was not much of a peek into reality, but by itself it was startling. All Japanese papers carried this official release from Imperial Headquarters on the Tokyo attack:

"The enemy planes invaded Japan from east of Chiba [a small city east of Tokyo]. The mainstay of the force attacked Tokyo, and the rest, about ten planes each, came over Chiba, Miyagi, Fukushima, and Iwate Prefecture. The enemy used his bombers from extremely varied angles, thereby obstructing the use of our radars. The fire bombing was carried out by one plane after another from various directions largely from an altitude of 3,000 to 4,000 meters, the lowest 1,000 meters."

Much later, freed of the restrictions of official censorship, the reporters of Japan's great newspapers were able to write what they had seen, experienced, and felt that night. One newspaperman wrote:

"That bright, starlit night will remain in the memory of all who witnessed it. Whole districts burned to the ground. Only here and there were walls of the rare stone buildings left standing.

"After the first bombs fell, clouds formed and were lit from below with a pink light. From them emerged Superfortresses, flying uncannily low above the centers of rapidly spreading conflagration. A B-29 exploded before our eyes like a magnesium tracer bullet, almost over the center of the city.

"The fire clouds kept creeping higher, and the tower of the Diet Building stood out black against the red sky. The city was as bright as at sunrise; clouds of smoke, soot, even sparks driven by the storm, flew over it. That night we thought the whole of Tokyo was reduced to ashes."

Another Japanese newspaperman wrote:

"There were many strange things after that raid. Victims were evacuated to private homes in a nearby good residential section. They were so pitiful that their hosts were kind and gave them all kinds of attention. Instead of being grateful, the slum people resented the fact that in war, while they were suffering, people should be having such luxuries as they couldn't dream of having even in peace. So they looted wholesale, and the police could do nothing about it. After that, people were evacuated not to private homes but to schools and public buildings. Soon the B-29's bombed the good sections of the city also, and then all of the people were in the same boat."

But on March 10th and 11th of 1945 even the unprecedented steps taken by the Japanese editors and their publishers did not reveal fully the horror of what had taken place in Tokyo. The newspapers did not publish the shocking fact, for example, that nearly seventeen square miles of the industrial heartland of the city had been gutted, that only shells of buildings remained. Nor did they dare to write of the numbers of the dead, the burned and maimed. They did not write that within twenty-four hours the Japanese knew that at least eighty-four thousand people had died, that possibly another fifty to one hundred thousand also were no longer among the living. City officials who knew the slum area better than most confided that there was every chance that the final death toll, although exact figures were impossible, would reach a quarter of a million!

In the great earthquake of 1923, the earth shocks and subsequent fires caused—by official count—the death of approximately one hundred thousand people. Another 43,000 persons were missing, and at least 25,000 of this number finally were added to the death toll. The earthquake trapped tens of thousands of people beneath collapsed buildings, but the fire resulting from the catastrophe moved much slower than the enormous tidal wave of flame that rolled irresistibly through Tokyo during the early morning hours of March 10th, 1945. For so quickly did this fire move, so rapidly did it consume everything in its path, so swiftly did it snuff the life from its victims, that there was little time for the shock of the attack to be fully realized.

Not even the great British air assault of Operation Gomorrah in the summer of 1943, of which I wrote in detail in my book *The Night Hamburg Died*, so eluded description. It was committed to history by the German city's Police President. Then, too, Gomorrah was a sustained attack over a period of ten days and ten nights. There was time for shock to abate, for realization to sink deeply into the senses and memories of the people involved. There was time to assemble records and documents and to gather together the many facets of the story that led to a secret document which in explicit detail recorded the events that occurred during the terrible days and nights.

At the end of that period, twelve square miles of Hamburg had become a stomach-wrenching cemetery of dead.

In approximately *six hours*—nearly seventeen square miles of Tokyo were burned out, and more than 100,000 people killed.

It was too fast, the shock too great, to record in detail. Tokyo has been too beclouded by the flaming, boiling smoke of its own brief but savage gutting for the story to emerge without extensive research. Hamburg suffered a firestorm, several firestorms. The characteristics were observed, dissected, committed to records.

Not until I completed the research for this volume, with the assistance of Fred Saito in Japan, who pored over official Japanese records, talked to survivors, reached back into his own memory, was I sure that it was possible to recreate the full story of those hours in Tokyo.

Many years ago I went personally through the gutted area of the Japanese capital. I flew over the city, and saw the great scars on the face of the land. Rapid reconstruction along street fronts hid much of the devastated area from the man on foot; the view from an airplane is not restricted by this façade, and the wounds are stark and real.

I pored through volume after volume of the *United States Strategic Bombing Survey*. I went through reports of psychological studies on the effects of the attack on the Japanese. There were combat-organization histories to be studied, former B-29 pilots and crew members to interview.

I am especially indebted to the editors of *Impact* magazine, an official Army Air Force publication that carried the stamp of "Confidential" throughout its lifetime and which went out of publication when the Japanese formally surrendered in September 1945. A group of editors—Lt. Colonel Edward K. Thompson, Lt. Colonel Robert E. Girvin, Major Maitland A. Edey, and Captains Tom Prideaux, Peter B. Greenough, Gordon G. Macnab, and Hugh Fosburgh—made *Impact* the finest military publication ever put together, and brought to the continuing history and events of World War II brilliant new perspective. Much material in this book has leaned heavily on the detailed reporting and brilliant writing of *Impact*'s staff.

It would require extraordinary callousness, when reviewing the appalling carnage caused during World War II by the bombers of the American and British air forces, to attempt appraisal of the "worst" of all those attacks. Horror, after all, is horror no matter where one looks at it, and the human mind finally reaches its saturation point and cannot measure additional fear or suffering.

What the city of Hamburg suffered is unique unto itself, and it will never be known by any other people, no matter what their tribulations. Dresden lost many more people in a single night than died in Hamburg in ten flaming nights; yet survivors of Hamburg would gladly have chanced death in Dresden, if only to have been spared the continuing, unremitting savagery of *Gomorrah*.

And what of Berlin, where more than 25,000 people

died in a single, daylight raid by 2,500 heavy bombers of the Eighth Air Force? Or Toyama, which was 99 per cent burned out in a single B-29 attack? Or Hiroshima or Nagasaki?

By whatever name it is called, whatever city suffers, Hell is Hell.

Tokyo, of course, occupies (like Hamburg or Hiroshima) a special place on the long roll of cities that were trampled by explosives and fire. On three separate occasions Tokyo suffered what is known as the "sweep conflagration," the most devastating of all fires.

The firestorm is a living *thing* of flame. It creates unbelievable winds, temperatures of 1,500 degrees F.; it hurls its fire miles into the heavens. But it is self-contained. It burns in upon itself. The winds rush toward a common center and then shriek skyward. Fire-spread is only by the limited pace of radiated heat, and outside the perimeter, many hundreds of feet from the flames, it is possible to prevent the creeping outward movement. No one survives the interior of a firestorm; those who are beyond its reach, however, are assured of survival.

The sweep conflagration is a different breed of fire. It is a swollen, maddened thing running amuck. It is not self-contained, for it runs *before* the wind. It is like a steamroller hundreds of feet high and miles wide, roaring and shrieking as it moves in a high-crested wave, bending over along the edges.

Because it is so low to the ground in comparison to the firestorm, it feeds on richer oxygen along its blazing edges. It is *hotter* than the firestorm. In Tokyo the wall of flame hovering just above the heads of terrorized, fleeing human beings reached an unbelievable temperature of more than 1,800 degrees F.! It was so hot that *heat*—not fire—shot out for hundreds of feet and struck people down as though with a great invisible scythe.

This was the Hell of Tokyo.

This was the raid of March 9-10th, 1945, in which a possible toll of a quarter of a million human beings was exacted, resulting in nearly seventeen square miles of the heart of the city slashed by fire knives into unholy ruin.

There was another heavy incendiary attack two months later.

Nineteen square miles of Tokyo vanished as the great tidal wave of flame consumed almost everything in its path. Not nearly as many people fell victim. They had left Tokyo, abandoned their city to the B-29's, fled to the hills and mountains.

The people who survived the March 10th raid had a grim sameness about them. They were shocked into a world of retreat, drowning in a calamity too great for their senses to accept.

Some sat on the ground; some stood unmoving, like statues. They stared at the terrible, monstrous flatness where their city had been. They were not angry, or bitter, or even filled with hate. They had no emotions left; they were numb, mute.

They were just like the people who had miraculously survived Hamburg, or perhaps Berlin or Dresden. It might have been Nagoya, Osaka, or Kobe. Or perhaps Hiroshima, or Nagasaki.

It didn't matter, really.

Horror is the same everywhere.

1

STRATEGIC APPRAISAL

On August 14th, 1945, the military ruler of half a billion people and a land area encompassing nearly three million square miles admitted complete defeat and surrendered unconditionally to his opponents. The empire of Japan, which shortly before this surrender had reached the zenith of its conquests, had been shattered as a world power. Japan still possessed millions of well-equipped and well-trained soldiers. Her homeland knew not a single enemy soldier. She had more than ten thousand aircraft ready to pounce in a devastating suicide assault against an invasion fleet.

Yet, Japan surrendered. This move was forced upon her as the result of a vast and well-coordinated effort conducted with steadily increasing violence that utilized well the enormous industrial resources of the United States.

"Fully recognizing the indispensable contributions of other arms," stated General H. H. Arnold in his report of November 12th, 1945, to the Secretary of War, "I feel that air power's part may fairly be called decisive.

"The collapse of Japan has vindicated the whole strategic concept of the offensive phase of the Pacific war. Viewed broadly and simply, that strategy has been to advance air power, both land- and carrier-based, to the point where the full fury of crushing air attack could be loosed on Japan itself, with the possibility that such attack would bring about the defeat of Japan without invasion, and with the certainty that it would play a vital role in preparation for and cooperation with, an invasion.

"No invasion was necessary."

Because the strategic bombing campaign directed against the Japanese homeland—as well as against targets in Manchuria, in China, and throughout southeast Asia—differed so greatly from the strategic bombing campaigns of Europe, it is most important to illuminate those differences. In my previous book, *The Night Hamburg Died,* I presented some details of the vast organization of the Royal Air Force's Bomber Command which led to a series of massive air assaults against German industrial zones and individual cities. It should be noted that the very nature of Britain's defense position in relation to the continent of Europe supported the creation of such a heavy bomber force. The ultimate targets were obvious, the routes to and from them could be planned years ahead of time, and logistical support of such a program is infinitely easier when the problem can be solved right "in your own backyard."

In terms of preparation and buildup for an extensive, heavy-bomber campaign, the British Isles were ideal. It is true that they were hampered by notoriously bad weather, but electronic devices aided enormously in overcoming this difficulty. Airfields were plentiful, defenses superb, and the organization exceedingly well-knit and capable of meeting its requirements.

The same situation existed with the Eighth Bomber Command, which functioned in brilliant coordination with the British. It was a bombardment campaign in which all the essentials were well delineated beforehand; the problems were great, but the path toward their solution was never in doubt.

This was, unfortunately, not the case in the vast reaches of the Pacific and in Asia. At the beginning of the war the suggestion of an immediate heavy bombardment campaign against the Japanese homeland would likely have been met with derision. The VLR (Very Long Range) program that was placed in planning soon after the war began despaired of solving the fantastic problems.

There existed no logistic organization—it had to be

created, and then sustained over one-way distances of at least ten thousand miles.

There existed not a single airfield on which to base giant bombers, which at the time did not even exist! The Flying Fortresses and Liberators of the European daylight precision campaign were not large enough; these were exceeded in size by the British Lancasters and Halifaxes, but these great heavyweights could not compare in range with the Boeing B-29 Superfortress, which was hurriedly nourished from the drawing boards into production. The B-29 was not just another bomber, it was the first intercontinental raider; it was the first bomber to incorporate "aerodynamic design breakthroughs"; and it employed radical new systems, such as completely electronic outfitting, radar bombing, remote-control turrets, which could be fired interchangeably among the gunners, pressurization which made operation possible at 38,000 feet without oxygen masks.

Halifax

In the early days of the Pacific war, it was as remote as a spaceship that could travel to Mars.

And yet, even in those grim times, our air strategists in Washington recognized that without such a machine the war against Japan would be a prohibitively long, costly, bloody campaign—which is exactly what the Japanese had planned. On our side, if the B-29 could be rushed through in its development, production, training, and overseas deployment—while forces of the three services secured bases within B-29 reach of the Japanese mainland—then the issue would no longer be in doubt. The protection of great distance would be ripped away from the factories and cities. The heart of the great Japanese fighting machine could be pierced, with all the catastrophic consequences.

We would not be forced to engage the millions of soldiers in terrible land campaigns, or even to commit ourselves to the bloody invasion of Japan.

The B-29 was more than a bomber aiming at the heart of Japan. If successful, it would change the entire concept of war. But all this, as the Japanese hurled us back across the Pacific and in Asia, lay very far in a cloudy, distant future.

The war that was fought against the Japanese Empire fell into three general phases. First there was the period of defense, from the attack against Pearl Harbor and the simultaneous sweep of enemy forces throughout the Pacific and Asia. Much of this period was a time of black despair, as our forces were hurled back with heavy losses. Then came the battle of Midway in June of 1942, when for the first time the United States Navy struck back, and in a successful divebombing attack smashed and sank four of Japan's great aircraft carriers. This began the "offensive-defensive" period, or "holding" phase.

The problem now was to keep the Japanese from extending their already enormous gains. We entered into limited offensives (Guadalcanal), but our major intent in the war against Japan was to deploy men and matériel so that we could begin the program to reach the Japanese mainland. Unfortunately—for us, but to the good fortune of the Japanese—the war in Europe of necessity claimed the highest priorities, and the Japanese were spared for a time the enormous output of our factories.

But in mid-1944 the war in Europe was already resolved. It was not yet won, but there could be no doubt of the outcome. The battle areas were reduced steadily. The African continent was clear. Our forces were on the European continent; the Russians were storming against the Germans from the East.

The VLR (Very Long Range) program, initiated on paper several years before, began to assume substance. We had fought our way through the enemy's perimeter to capture islands, rushed through a construction program of airbases, poured in supplies and manpower, and now it was time to go on the offensive in Asia. The cities of Japan became the primary objective of a rapidly growing fleet of great B-29 bombers.

On the morning of December 7th, 1941, when the last Japanese airplane departed Pearl Harbor, some sailors picked up several leaflets that had fluttered down on the flaming wreckage of Oahu. They read: "Goddam Americans all to go hell." Period.

This was Japan's concept of how to wage psychological warfare against the men of our armed forces. It proved one thing immediately: while we knew precious little of the Japanese, they knew even less of us.

On the first day of World War II, the Japanese struck in a massive, brilliantly coordinated assault across a front that stretched for ten thousand miles. The United States lost two-thirds of its aircraft in the Pacific theater. So effective was the attack against Pearl Harbor and its environs that Hawaii was completely useless as a source of supply and reinforcement for the Philippines. And on those islands, already beleaguered by Japanese land, sea, and air forces, the enemy's attacks steadily whittled down our remaining air strength until it was no more than an annoyance to a victorious foe.

History is not at all kind to us in a review of those early days. Japan controlled as much of the vast China mainland and its resources as she deemed feasible at the time. She had captured Guam and Wake. She threw us out of the Netherlands East Indies. Singapore fell in humiliating defeat, and the Japanese broke the back of British sea power. Within a few months apprehension in Australia turned to terror as Australian cities were brought under direct air attack. Japanese planes swarmed almost uncontested against northern New Guinea, New Ireland, the Admiralties, New Britain, and the Solomons. The Japanese occupied Kavieng, Rabaul, and Bougainville, thereby directly threatening the precarious supply lines from the United States, and giving the Japanese potential springboards for the occupation of Australia itself.

During these long and dreary months the Japanese did much more than merely humiliate us in our meetings throughout the Pacific. They beat us—pure and simple.

The Japanese had a grandiose scheme that befitted their spirit of invincibility. They were supported in their drives by centuries of victorious tradition, their plans were fostered by myths and fairy tales, and they were bolstered by years of one-track tradition. With this background, and their immediate, overwhelming successes, the Japanese were absolutely convinced of victory. They were certain that all the Pacific and much of Asia would fall within their "Greater East Asia Coprosperity Sphere."

And yet, even as all this took place, the plans were being drawn to eliminate the effects of Japan's shock offensives. It is truly astonishing to realize that even during the height of their steamroller offensive, the Japanese never really had the strength to achieve ultimate victory.

The overwhelming numerical superiority which the Japanese enjoyed—largely by destruction of our own forces with relative impunity—began to disappear. By the spring of 1943 there had taken place a definite, ominous shifting in the power balance. The qualitative inferiority we had suffered was almost vanished. We began to enjoy, despite the terrible drain of European commitments, the fruits of our tremendous industrial organization. From then on the Japanese were fighting not for land, but for their very lives.

The majority of the Japanese military hierarchy never recognized this reality. They basked in their successes of the early months of war and reveled in their spirit of invincibility. Any losses were only temporary. They counted their blessings in raw materials and industries of the lands they occupied, and prepared for the glorious future.

They did not realize that because American industry was never a target of their plans, they had already lost the war. But Japanese industry was the very crux of our strategic plans.

The Japanese high command believed absolutely that their factories and cities would never know heavy air attack—and this was the Achilles' heel of Japanese strategy. Their tacticians and strategists fought the war entirely out of the rule books. The terrible power of the B-29 assault left them dumbfounded. They had never prepared for strategic air attack, they were incapable of effective countermeasures.

The Japanese failed because their men and officers were inferior, not in courage, *but in the intelligent use of courage.* In a predicted situation which could be handled in an orthodox manner, the Japanese were always competent and often they were resourceful. Under the shadow of frustration, however, the obsession of personal honor blinded the Japanese to reality and extinguished ingenuity.

Because they themselves lacked a formula for strategic air power, the Japanese never considered the possibility that it would be used against them.

Japan was terribly vulnerable. Her far-flung supply lines were comparable to delicate arteries nurtured by a bad heart. The value of her captured land masses and the armed forces which defended them were in direct proportion to the ability of her shipping to keep them supplied, to keep the forces mobile, and to bring back to Japan the materials to keep her factories running. Destroy the shipping, and Japan for all practical purposes would be four islands without an empire.

Four islands on which were cities made to order for destruction by fire.

This became the plan. Destroy the shipping and burn the cities. We did exactly that.

"Even before one of our B-29's dropped its atomic bomb on Hiroshima," continues General Arnold's report to the Secretary of War, "Japan's military situation was hopeless. Without attempting to minimize the appalling and far-reaching results of the atomic bomb, we have good reason to believe that its actual use provided a way out for the Japanese government. The fact is that the Japanese could not have held out long, because they had lost control of their air. They could not offer effective opposition to our bombardment, and so could not prevent the destruction of their cities and industries. . . . "

The B-29's loosed an incredible torrent of fire on Japan. Her ability to continue the war collapsed amid the ashes of her scarred and gutted urban centers. The two atomic bombs contributed *less than 3 per cent* of the destruction visited upon the industrial centers of Japan. But they gave the Japanese, so preoccupied with saving face, an excuse and a means of ending a long, futile war with honor intact.

A modern industrial nation such as Japan would never have admitted defeat unless her industrial potential had been hopelessly weakened, the morale of her people seriously affected, and her isolation from the essentials necessary to wage war rendered virtually complete by blockade and the destruction of her Navy and merchant fleet. The fanatical Japanese would never have accepted the crushing terms of the Potsdam ultimatum merely because of the awesome power bearing down upon them.

"The Japanese Army was still capable of inflicting heavy casualties on an invading force," wrote General Arnold. "The Kamikaze Corps had shown its capabilities in the Philippines and Okinawa campaigns and was preparing for an even greater effort against our invasion. Yet the Japanese acknowledged defeat because air attacks, both actual and potential, had made possible the destruction of their capability and will for further resistance."

June 15th, 1944, was the day that the American long-range campaign to burn the guts out of Japan reached level ground and shifted into high gear. That was the day that China-based B-29's poured explosives into the great Yawata steel works. A long distance away, marines stormed ashore on the island of Saipan, and assured that the B-29's would have their final stepping stone for the massive bombardment of the Japanese homeland.

"It was the day that the Japanese high command had to admit," wrote the editors of *Impact* in their final issue, "to themselves at least, that their beautiful dream of insulation had turned into an horrendous nightmare.

"Having taken the Marianas, we were finally in a position, with the B-29, to wage a strategic war of attrition against the Japanese empire. From here on in, the increase of Allied strength would go hand in hand with the deterioration of the Japanese capacity to fight back. We were ready to launch a vicious spiral of destruction from which there could not possibly be any escape. If the Japanese backed up farther, we would advance more quickly. If they chose to stand and fight, we would destroy them and have so much less to cope with later on. It was as simple as that. It was as simple as that because the Allies had amassed a power that was titanic. The Japanese could not stand up to it and there was no place they could go to get away from it. They had no immovable object to place against the irresistible force. Eventually they had just one final choice—give up or be destroyed."

The burning of Japan's cities became assured in December of 1943 with the decision to institute the VLR—the Very Long Range campaign that would use the radical new aerial weapon, the B-29, against the enemy's homeland.

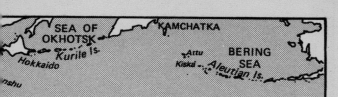

SEA OF
OKHOTSK
KAMCHATKA

Kurile Is.
BERING
SEA

Attu
Hokkaido
Kiska
Aleutian Is.

nshu

NORTH PACIFIC
OCEAN

Midway

Wake

Hawaiian Islands

Pearl Harbor

Marshall Is.

Gilbert Islands

New Hebrides

ty Is.
Fiji Is.

PACIFIC THEATER

Nautical miles

| 0 | 600 | 1200 | 1800 |

NEW
ZEALAND

2

THE VLR PROGRAM

For the air strategist, no one thing is so important as *range*—the ability of a bombing airplane to take off from its home base, carry a load of bombs to the target, and then return to base. Range, however, is an elusive thing. An airplane may have a range with a bay filled with bombs of 3,000 miles. But that does not always mean that the airplane can fly to a target 1,500 miles from its home airfield and return.

More specifically defined, the effective range of a bombing airplane is reduced to its practical combat *radius of action*. For example, the airplane that can fly for 3,000 miles, carrying bombs to the halfway point, must use much of its fuel for requirements other than reaching its target: running up its engines on the ground, climbing to cruising altitude with a heavy bomb load, compensating for errors along its route. Beyond this, a fuel reserve must be provided for errors in navigation, engines that may not operate at peak efficiency, and the effects of shifting winds that may add many miles to the flight.

The result is that an airplane with a range of 3,000 miles may have a combat radius of only 1,200 miles.

When our strategists began to detail their plans for the destruction of Japanese factories and cities, they could tell easily enough the necessary performance of the weapon they would employ. If you have a chain of airfields along a line north and south of Chengtu in China, and draw an arc with a compass extending outward for 1,600 miles, most of Japan's industries fall within that arc.

If the point of the compass is placed on the island of Saipan, the arc encompasses all of Kyushu, Shikoku, and the most important cities and factories of the main island of Honshu. Saipan, with all its problems of construction, however, promised infinitely simpler logistics requirements. It was much closer to the United States; the line of supply would be direct. To the air strategist, Saipan could become a vital fulcrum for the campaign against Japan. The trouble with this plan, however, was that our hopes for fighting our way closer to the Japanese islands did not call for Saipan to be attacked before 1946, while airfields in China within radius of action of Japan would be available at least two years before then.

What about the weapon? In this respect the strategic campaign as it matured was fraught with controversy. Flight tests showed that the great four-engined raider could carry ten tons of bombs over a range of 3,000 miles, or fly 4,400 miles without the weight of the bombs. A 3,500-mile range meant that the B-29, flying from Saipan, could bring the targets of Japan within its reach—a radius of action from Saipan of 1,600 miles. On the basis of these computations, there would be just 300 miles of flying as a safety margin.

This may appear to be an ample figure, but in actual flying time it is perilously brief.

In November of 1943 an Army Air Force general wrote that "the B-29 airplane was thought out and planned as a high altitude, long-range bomber to attack Japan, her cities and industrial keypoints."

When those words were written, it seemed obvious that this was the natural mission for the B-29. The truth is, however, that the original requirement for this great bomber had nothing at all to do with the Japanese homeland; the prewar Air Corps was more concerned about territory much closer to our own border than a nation lying at the far end of the Pacific Ocean.

It was during the period of 1938-1941 that airpower strategists began to develop the concept of hemisphere defense. The justification for building the four-engined B-17 and B-24 bombers did not include striking at German cities, but rather the defense of our immediate shores—long-range reconnaissance and attacks against enemy fleets attempting to invade either the United States directly, or its possessions.

B-17 Flying Fortress

Then it became only too obvious that Germany, to say nothing of Japan and Italy, was developing ominous plans for movement into South America. Germany showed intentions of pursuing a path of economic involvement, infiltration into labor groups and government, and then direct military intervention. Thus the Air Corps looked south with increasing concern; from South America German bombers could strike not only at the Panama Canal, but at industrial objectives within the continental United States.

The need for "counter-air operations" became pressing, and plans were drawn to create a new air weapon that, based in the United States, could effectively attack any German foothold in South America. The specifications for the new aircraft, which called initially for a radius of action of 2,000 miles, led to two airplanes—the Boeing B-29 Superfortress and the Convair B-32 Dominator. (Technical difficulties so hampered the development of the B-32 that it was produced only in small numbers, and saw but limited combat in the Pacific in World War II.)

Thus, the primary purpose of the B-29 was not to attack the enemy in his homeland, but rather to destroy his foothold in the Americas. However, as events have proved with our other bombing aircraft, the Air Corps was infused with the doctrine of offensive air operations, and to the leaders of that Air Corps there existed not a shred of doubt that the B-29 would fulfill its ultimate role as a destroyer of cities. Indeed, in 1939, when the airplane was still on its drawing board, Colonel (later General) Carl A. Spaatz suggested that the bomber might well end up being based in Luzon, Siberia, or the Aleutians to strike at Japanese industry.

In the early days of World War II, the danger that Britain might fall to the onslaught of German arms led Air Corps strategists to draw up operational plans for attacking German industry from bases in North Africa. Underlying the whole story of the B-29, of course, was the unquestionable logic that it is far wiser and more efficient to destroy the sources of munitions, i.e., the home factories, than to keep on attacking the products.

It was in the spring of 1941 that the VLR program first assumed its definite outlines. American and British military staffs met in top-secret conferences to plan for coordinated activities should the United States become embroiled in the European war. At this time the VLR bomber—exceeding anything else planned by either of the two countries—was anticipated as the most devastating weapon of the United States. And by September of 1941, when the first specific war plans were drawn, the defensive role of the B-29 had been cast aside, and its new mission as a destroyer of factories and cities within the enemy's home country clearly established.

As envisioned in this original plan of operations, by 1944 there would be twenty-four groups of B-29's and B-32's operating from bases in Great Britain and Egypt to strike at Germany. If the planes could be spared, an additional two groups would be sent to Luzon to attack Japan.

History establishes that the war against Japan insofar as priorities were concerned ran second to the fight against Germany; this was a doctrine established clearly before Pearl Harbor. Despite the crushing Japanese successes in the early months of the war, the Army Air Forces did not vary from this position. The conflict with Japan would be primarily a defensive war in which naval forces would predominate, and only after Germany was defeated would we turn our full and combined attentions to wiping out the remainder of the Japanese Empire.

As late as the spring of 1943, the concept of the B-29 and B-32 being used almost exclusively for attack against Germany went unchallenged within the A.A.F. As plans were developed, the great bombers would shuttle between England and North Africa, hurling ten-ton loads of bombs from each plane into targets.

In March of 1943, Major General Ira C. Eaker of the Eighth Air Force, whose responsibility was development of final plans for the CBO (Combined Bomber Offensive) against German targets, requested of the Pentagon a tentative deployment schedule of B-29 groups. Washington, however, refused definite commitments at this time, or later. Not until December of 1944, only seven months after the first B-29 went into combat, did AAF Headquarters make its final and definite decision that the VLR Program would operate with Japan as the objective.

But the heavy bombardment of Europe was not the only task for which the B-29's were sought. In April of 1943, for example, the Antisubmarine Command tried to secure twenty-four of the great bombers. Also, the Navy had obtained from the A.A.F. long-range B-24's for reconnaissance and patrol, and they tried to acquire the heavy bombers. This request was an occasion of curt and angry comment from the A.A.F. Behind the scenes, the Navy protested bitterly the crash priorities for production granted the B-29; Navy authorities had claimed that this effort interfered with their own requirements, and that the B-29 should be relegated to a lesser production priority status. In view of these actions, the A.A.F. on July 7th, 1943, in a sharp retort stated that "the Army Air Forces will not discuss the allocation of B-29's to the Navy."

THE WEAPON

The *Manhattan Project* that produced the atomic bomb for the United States was considered the single most expensive research and development effort in American history. The total for this development over a span of only three years came to two billion dollars—even in time of the war a fantastic outlay for a single program.

Before the first B-29 took to the air, on June 29th, 1943, however, the Army Air Forces had already spent or allocated to be spent for the B-29 program the incredible sum of three billion dollars!

It is not thought of as such, but the B-29 represents one of the biggest military gambles of all time. It was developed in absolute secrecy by more than 750 engineers who worked in secrecy for more than two years. This engineering effort never diminished; a year after the B-29 dropped its first bombs, a thousand engineers were still working day and night to effect improvements that would increase its combat value.

The B-29 presented more problems for the aviation industry and the Army Air Forces than they had ever known before. Its size alone was a major consideration—in engineering, in production, and in testing. Time was a terrible hurdle to overcome. It meant producing the biggest bomber in the least time with a minimum of second-guessing and redesigning.

Yet, because men gambled fortunes and careers, labored unselfishly day and night, and—some of them—gave their lives, the dream became reality, and a war that promised to last until 1948 was ended three years sooner, with incalculable savings in lives, blood, and matériel. Much of the credit for this success belongs to Major General K. B. Wolfe, Brigadier General Laverne Saunders, and their staffs.

The first B-29—the first of three XB-29 prototypes—took to the air in 1942. Working on a crash basis, the airplane was tested, modified, and retested again and again, so that by June 29th, 1943, the first production B-29 was in the air and accepted officially by the Army Air Forces. Colonel Leonard Harmon flew it from its factory for delivery to the Army; weeks later, Harmon was touring China by air in an accelerated airfield survey. He knew the B-29 better than any pilot flying, and his experience in the Superfortress was vital in making correct decisions for a massive airfield-construction program around Changsha.

The B-29 was the first American bomber that was designed for combat operations at great altitudes—above 30,000 feet. Because of this need for endurance at altitude, engineers built into the enormous airplane pressurized flight compartments and an air-heating system. On the long flights the crews were free of the necessity of wearing their oxygen masks and cumbersome heated flying suits. Cruising toward their targets at 30,000 feet, they operated at an atmospheric pressure of 8,000 feet. Approaching the target, each man donned his oxygen mask and flight-suit and the bomber was depressurized to avoid explosive decompression from skin punctures of enemy bullets or flak.

But the most astonishing innovation of all was the central-fire-control (CFC) system, an electronic-computer-operated defensive system that took the guesswork out of gunnery. Because its speed, altitude and range were greater than any fighter planes of that time, the B-29 would have to fly combat operations without fighter escort, in defiance of the bitterly taught lessons of Europe.

The airplane had five gun turrets, two on top of the fuselage, two on the bottom, and one in the tail. The upper forward turret had four .50 caliber machine guns, and the other three fuselage positions had two guns each. In the tail was a 20-mm. cannon, flaked with .50 caliber machine guns. The total armament was therefore twelve machine guns and a cannon.

The gunners were at five sighting stations completely separate from the gun turrets. The bombardier served as nose gunner, a top gunner sighted out of a plexiglass dome between the two upper turrets, two side gunners sat in hemispherical plexiglass blisters, and the tail gunner sighted from his station under the tail fin. The stations were so arranged as to eliminate all blind spots, and there was no quarter of the sky from which an attacking fighter could approach unseen.

A turret-switching system enabled one gunner to operate several turrets if the airplane was attacked from a single direction, or if a gunner was killed. Selection of additional turrets required no more effort than flicking a switch. It was a revolutionary system that at once made obsolete even the powerful defensive fire of the B-17.

To augment the system, the gunners relied upon an electronic computer that instantaneously calculated not only the speed and distance of attacking fighters, but also made all necessary computations for the effects of gravity deflection, wind, temperature, and altitude.

A measure of the effectiveness of this fire-control system in keeping Japanese fighters at their distance is that in the first six months of combat operations (out of China) only fifteen B-29's were lost to enemy fighters in air-to-air combat. To obtain these victories, it cost the Japanese 102 fighters definitely destroyed, 87 probably destroyed, and another 156 seriously damaged.

There was also much to be said for the amazing structural integrity of the giant airplane. Perhaps the most bizarre night-fighter mission for any American pilot fell to Lieutenant Arthur C. Shepherd, pilot of a P-61 Black Widow, who was ordered to shoot down a derelict B-29 that was flying wild over the island of Iwo Jima. The airplane had almost been torn apart in the air over Japan. An anti-aircraft shell smashed through the fuselage, tore a three-foot hole in the pilot's compartment, killed the pilot, destroyed all radio equipment, jammed the bomb-bay doors closed, and riddled the airplane with shrapnel. The copilot was badly wounded and bleeding, but struggled to fly the crippled B-29 back to its base.

On the return, Shepherd in the P-61 spotted the shattered Superfortress and led the cripple to Iwo Jima where the crew could bail out. On the first run across the island eight of the eleven-man crew tumbled into space. The copilot brought her around, put the airplane on automatic pilot, and then jumped with the remainder of the crew.

P-61 Black Widow

Left in the airplane was the body of the dead pilot and the full load of bombs. The B-29 was no longer simply an abandoned airplane; it was a terrible bomb on wings that could conceivably crash and explode Iwo Jima itself.

As the ghost droned along, Shepherd brought his Black Widow into position to shoot the derelict out of the sky. He had plenty of armament for the job—four 20-mm.

cannon and four .50 caliber machine guns, all firing in a concentrated stream.

But the B-29 refused to go down. "As soon as we cleared the island," Shepherd said, "we started firing with all eight guns. Our first burst hit the left outboard engine, which began to smoke and then to flame.

"The loss of an engine swung the B-29 back toward Iwo. We held fire until it cleared the island again, then gave it everything we had. Altogether we poured 564 rounds of .50 caliber bullets and 320 rounds of 20-mm. cannon shells into the staggering B-29.

"We were flying close enough to see where practically every round was hitting, and we wondered how long the big bomber could keep on taking it. Finally, just as it began to seem as if the B-29 would keep on flying forever, it headed downward and plunged into the sea."

The airplane was big by anyone's standards—a wingspan of 142 feet and a length of just under 100 feet. Under full combat weight, it lifted from the ground at 135,000 pounds, carrying as much gasoline as a railroad tanker, with its heavy bomb load in two large, separate bays. The bomb load was variable, and it could include, for example, as many as *forty* 500-pound bombs. Despite this weight, the airplane's four engines, each of 2,200 horsepower and driving a four-bladed propeller, gave it a combat-loaded top speed of 361 miles per hour.

With its 15,000 feet of electric wiring and electrically operated accessories, the B-29 was accepted with open arms by ground crews as an electrical engineer's dream—although it could easily have been a maintenance man's nightmare. It required 129 electric motors, 29 motor-generators, and 7 generators just to keep the B-29 flying, and each of these had to be designed for its specific job and built to stand up under varying conditions of climate and temperature with a minimum of care and replacement. There were more than 55,000 numbered parts in every Superfortress.

Five enormous factories were devoted exclusively to B-29 production, and by the close of 1944 the combined production rate of these plants was exceeding six airplanes every twenty-four hours. The B-29 was an expensive machine, but as mass production became reality, costs went down. The first airplane cost exactly $3,392,396.60. The production cost per airplane in January of 1945 was down to $600,000.

The problems of training were no simpler than those of production. Speed again was the imperative factor. General Wolfe believed that he could eliminate existing methods of bringing the B-29 to a state of combat readiness; he devised a system by which it became practical to work the "bugs" out of the new airplane simultaneously with production and training, and therefore he could save considerable time in the usual long jump that was required from factory to combat. He predicted that he could save as much as six months in the entire program (when six months meant everything) if he took the airplanes as they came off the assembly line and put them through strains equivalent to those of combat at the same time that organization and training was in progress for the global Twentieth Air Force that would receive the B-29's.

The Pentagon gambled with Wolfe, and the authorization went out. It was in this fashion that the 58th Wing, and later the Twentieth Bomber Command, came into existence. By the time it was ready to ferry its aircraft to the China-Burma-India theater, the Twentieth Bomber Command was loaded with combat-experienced crews, yet Wolfe hadn't resorted to the practice of raiding active combat theaters for these personnel. He selected men who had completed their bombing missions, finished their rest periods at home, and were ready to return to battle.

Thus when the first B-29's moved out of the United States toward the continent of Asia, the great bombers were flown and crewed by men who knew bombers, who knew long-range flying, and who knew the enemy.

The B-29 was ready to go to war; time was beginning to run out for Tokyo and Japan's other cities.

3

TESTING THE WEAPON

On June 15th, 1944, the Japanese suffered two simultaneous blows from the forces of the United States—and each spelled disaster in flaming, bomb-punctuated letters. On this day some fifty B-29 raiders of the Twentieth Bomber Command struck at the Imperial Iron and Steel Works at Yawata in Kyushu, southernmost of the Japanese home islands. On the same day, in the Pacific Ocean, the 2nd and 4th Marine Divisions smashed ashore on the island of Saipan.

The Yawata attack was the first blow struck against the Japanese inner zone with VLR bombers operating from China bases; the invasion of Saipan was the first step in a move that would provide bases to support more effectively the accelerating program to burn out the heart of Japan.

It would make for dramatic reading to write here that the B-29 operations from China bases were brilliantly planned and as brilliantly executed, a project rushed through against all obstacles with the single purpose of destroying Japanese industry. But this simply isn't true. Political considerations just as much as military necessity brought the B-29 into the Chinese mainland, and the subsequent chapters of this vast and costly effort simply do not reveal anything even remotely approaching success.

In mid-1943, China was in desperate straits. Japanese armies held as much of Chinese territory as they desired; instead of wasting their energies in pushing further into the vast hinterland, they consolidated their gains in the ex-

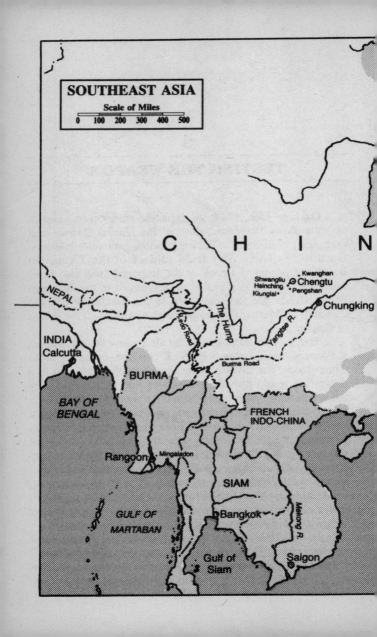

hausted country, stripping it of its few precious resources. In Burma, the deteriorating tactical situation was both dangerous and embarrassing to the Chungking government.

Indeed, on all counts, China was in so critical a position that the collapse of all resistance seemed certain. For months Chiang Kai-shek had demanded of President Roosevelt an intensified aerial campaign under the direction of Major General Claire Channault. In January of 1943 great promises were made to the Chinese, but, as states the *Official History of the A.A.F. in World War II*, "performance had fallen far short of goals."

On August 8th, 1943, the Combined Planning Staff (CPS) completed its plans for the future conduct of the war in the Pacific and Asia. The ultimate goal, of course, was the heavy attack by air upon Japanese cities—"an overwhelming bomber offensive preparatory to a final invasion." But as the CPS participants saw it, all operations in China and Burma would have to be intensified, and Hong Kong was to be recaptured so as to serve as the invasion port for a flood of supplies. To do this meant that first the Navy and the A.A.F. would have to seize and maintain a complete superiority in the China Sea. But because of Japanese naval strength, this effort must of necessity wait until the Central and Southwest Pacific areas had been won over by our forces.

Under this projected schedule, the Carolines (Truk Island) would have to be reduced, and the invasion of the Marinas (Guam, Saipan, Rota, Tinian) would not take place until sometime in 1946. Thus CPS estimated that the heavy-bomber offensive from the Asian mainland against Japan could not even begin until 1947!

The Joint Chiefs of Staff did not take long to file away these plans and begin to make their own moves toward an accelerated offensive in the Pacific. But never did hopes for attack against the Japanese mainland wane; indeed, they enjoyed the full support of the President. In 1943 the Committee of Operations Analysts had prepared an "analysis of strategic targets in Japan"—the destruction of which could reduce the anticipated lifetime of the war by several years (as ultimately it did).

Further details of the controversy between the Chinese

leader and American officials become too tedious for their appearance in these pages, but suffice it to say that at the November, 1943, Cairo Conference of Allied leaders, Chiang Kai-shek flatly threatened to take his country completely out of the war unless China was to receive, and at once, greater support from her Allies.

It was at this point that "political and strategic considerations" joined forces; first, it was necessary to bring to China the support that Chiang demanded, and second, the rapid rate of B-29 production encouraged the concept of a shorter war in the Far East. There would be no point in the Pacific from which the B-29's could reach Honshu in 1944 (this, too, was changed), according to plans, but it appeared that by October of 1944 ten groups of twenty-eight B-29's each could be ready for operations within China. Whatever the considerations, the signal was given to go ahead.

The final plan for bases called for advance airfields; B-29's would fly from their permanent bases in India to these advance fields, and stage through them for the flights to Japan. In January of 1944, General Wolfe and General Saunders flew to India for a firsthand check on the progress of the major fields.

"We wanted runways," said Wolfe in disgust. "We found a bunch of Indians making mud pies."

Wolfe turned to General Stilwell, the area ground-forces commander, for help—fast. "Vinegar Joe" Stilwell came through. He ordered engineers off the Ledo Road and turned them over to Wolfe.

"They came with a battery of concrete mixers, and put on the damnedest exhibition of instantaneous concrete laying you ever saw," said the astonished and delighted bomber-force commander.

Four great bomber fields were to be built in the Chengtu area—Pengshan, Kwanghan, Kiunglai, and Hsinching. Two hundred thousand Chinese laborers would work on the fields. In addition to the bomber fields that cost one billion Chinese dollars each, fighter fields were to be built at Shwangliu, Pungchachen, and Fungwhangshan.

But difficulties arose constantly, and before the project was completed, more than a half-million Chinese were hacking out the big runways and dispersal areas. It was a construction effort sufficient to make engineers tear out their hair. One example is related by Lt. Colonel Carey L. O'Brien, Jr.:

"Every coolie brought along a little wheelbarrow. The wheelbarrows squeaked. Thousands of squeaking wheelbarrows can get on the nerves, so one day when the Chinese were out having their lunch of rice our engineer had one of his boys grease all the axles.

"When the coolies came back they picked up their wheelbarrows and started to work. No squeak. They immediately put the wheelbarrows down and went home. The engineer called an interpreter and asked what was the matter. He was told: "No squeak in wheelbarrows means devil will come. Squeak keeps devil away. No squeak, plenty of devil—and no work!' So they had to rub all the grease off the wheelbarrow axles."

A B-29 rapid-supply system went into effect between Casablanca, the main shipping terminus, and Karachi, India. In a period of two months, twenty-five C-54 four-engined transports over a 16,000-mile supply route, carried

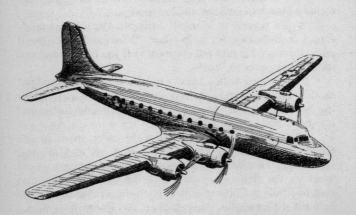

C-54

1,254 persons and a thousand tons of cargo—600 spare engines, radar parts, gunner blisters, auxiliary tanks, and other cargo.

From India, however, the B-29's had to carry their own essentials to their forward bases in China in order for them to bomb Japan. The wear and tear on the airplanes was fantastic. They carried not only fuel and spare parts, but their bombs, oil, engines, food, ammunition, guns, maintenance equipment, cooks and food, ad infinitum.

"It was a hell of a way to run a railroad," commented one bomber pilot. "For every combat mission we flew, we had to make six round-trip flights over the Hump. We were wearing out those B-29's."

There were some grandiose concepts entertained about the strength of the new forces. Originally, the A.A.F. planned to use the B-29's as a mobile force, free of any combat theater assignment, and able to rush to any area where their need was most urgent. "The power of these new bombers is so great," said General George C. Marshall, U.S. Army Chief of Staff, "that the Joint Chiefs of Staff felt that it would be uneconomical to confine the Superfortresses to a single theater. These bombers, therefore, will remain under the centralized control of the Joint Chiefs of Staff with a single commander, General Arnold, acting as their agent in directing their bombing operations throughout the world. The planes will be treated as major task forces in the same manner as naval task forces are directed against specific objectives."

It looked fine on paper, and it was certainly eloquent—but it didn't work. As the guinea pig for the new concept, the 58th Wing encountered overwhelming problems. The B-29 was a giant bomber, but there just weren't any giant, fast, long-range transports available in any number. Unable to be sustained by complete air supply, the bombers had to turn to specialized repair depots to support the groups of bases. But what most effectively brought a quick end to the "task forces" concept was that the B-29 was so large and heavy that it could not operate from ordinary runways, but demanded construction beyond that necessary to accommodate the lighter B-17's and B-24's.

THE B-29 GOES TO WAR

Despite all these formidable obstacles, and a further delay in the forecast operational schedules, by June 5th, 1944, the B-29 was ready for its combat debut. Ninety-eight of the great bombers took off from bases in India, headed for the Makasan railroad shops at Bangkok, Thailand (Siam). Two minutes after takeoff disaster struck. One bomber crashed and exploded, killing ten of the eleven crew members. Another twelve bombers aborted the raid because of mechanical and other difficulties. Over the target thick clouds drifted, obscuring the railroad repair shops. But alongside the clouds could be seen the outskirts of the city, and from a height of 25,000 feet, 77 B-29's dropped their bombs—five tons from each plane. Forty-eight managed, despite these difficulties as well as flak and fighters, to hit the target.

The chain of mishaps was not yet over. As the bombers cruised for home, they were caught in a 100-mile per hour gale of blinding yellow-purple clouds. Thirty bombers disappeared; hours later the reports of their whereabouts began to come in. Bombers had set down individually at sixteen different bases. One B-29 crashed in China; four men survived. Two other Superfortresses ditched in the Bay of Bengal; most of the crews were rescued.

It was not an auspicious combat debut, but the B-29 had cut its teeth.

Ten days later, on June 15th, 1944 (as the Marines stormed ashore at Saipan), 75 B-29's launched the first land-based strike at the Japanese home islands, aiming for the primary target of Yawata, and specifically the Imperial Iron and Steel Works. In terms of specific damage, the raid was unproductive. The airplanes carried only two tons of bombs each, and they met heavy clouds over the target. Fifty-five B-29's scattered their bombs around Yawata, Kokura, Moji, Tobata, and Shimonoseki. Not one bomb hit the steel works. Two planes attacked the secondary target of the Chinese port of Laoyao. Eleven planes aborted because of mechanical difficulties, two B-29's had to jettison their bombs just before reaching Yawata because of mechanical troubles. One bomber suffered engine failure on takeoff and crashed; one B-29 crash-landed in friendly territory. Still another went down at Heisiang in China and was burned by the Japanese. Two others vanished, their fate unknown.

It was not a profitable raid. Although the Japanese had failed to down any bombers, five planes were lost on this raid. In the Bangkok attack, four were lost. Nine planes were gone with little effect upon the enemy.

Yet the psychological effects of the attacks were electrifying. The reactions in Japan were stormy; the country's leaders had boasted of their nation's invulnerability to attack, and now the greatest bombers ever built had begun what obviously was to be a long campaign from the air.

To A.A.F. personnel, it was a time for cheering. No matter that in terms of results these attacks left much wanting. It was a beginning, the debut of a giant rushed through development, production, and training. The future looked brighter than ever before.

Operationally, however, enthusiasm proved no replacement for airplanes. Only seventeen bombers could be sent aloft for the third attack. Eleven struck at Sasebo, Yawata, Tobata and Omura, and two planes hit Hankow, China. All returned.

Then the picture changed. On July 29th, a daylight strike of 58 B-29's smashed the Showa steel works at Anshan, Manchuria. The results were spectacular. Even the Japanese acknowledged that a third of the plant had been totally destroyed; our intelligence went further and said the results were so effective that Anshan's coke ovens were out of commission permanently.

The B-29's continued to strike out at targets previously inaccessible to Allied air power. They hit other Japanese cities, and even reached out over the amazing distance, round trip, of 3,800 miles to attack oil installations in Sumatra. The results again left much to be desired, but the B-29 was proving it truly had seven-league boots, and what was learned from these attacks would be of enormous aid in future operations.

On August 20th, 1944, in a second raid against Yawata by seventy-five of the heavyweight bombers, the pilots found the Japanese fully alerted and ready for them.

Bombing results were "very good," but the anti-aircraft fire was intense and concentrated. Fighters had been assembled in the area and they attacked in great swarms. Twenty Japanese fighter planes went down, but the enemy was happy with the exchange. Ten B-29's were shot down by both the flak and fighters, and three others crash-landed at or near Allied bases. It was a costly raid.

The B-29's would operate from the Asian mainland over a period of ten months. The supply problem proved critical, for the heavy bombers were averaging only one mission every ten days, and that figure was exorbitantly wasteful of the powerful airplanes.

There were, however, some outstanding missions. In September of 1944 nearly 200 B-29's worked over the Showa steel works in Manchuria. A month later, in three missions to Formosa with a total of 198 airplanes, the bombers struck the great Okayama airplane assembly plant with 1,200 tons of high explosives; the plant suffered extensive damage, more than 100 planes were destroyed, 50 buildings burned to the ground, three ships in the harbor sunk, and the Einansho and Heito airfields partially demolished.

The Omura aircraft assembly plant on Kyushu took the brunt of several very heavy attacks, and the Japanese defended the vital target with intense anti-aircraft and fighter operations. In two raids, fifteen of the Superfortresses went down. Rangoon, Bangkok, Shanghai, Nanking, Hankow, Dairen, Singapore, Saigon, Amoy, Fuchow, Kuala Lumpur, Patuarang, Mingaladon, Mukden, and other targets were struck. Many of these raids evoked violent measures by the Japanese, as proved by their resorting to suicide tactics. Several times fighters deliberately rammed the B-29's (and sometimes the sturdy Superfortresses returned to base, wings and engines smashed, but still flying and under control).

Missions were flown over ranges of nearly 4,000 miles, testifying repeatedly to the tremendous endurance and reach of the new aerial weapon. And there were no doubts as to the effectiveness of the fire-control system. Single B-29's on reconnaissance missions dared the Japanese to do their worst, and the enemy responded. A B-29 flown by Captain J. C. Eigenmann on a flight over Honshu was attacked for more than a full hour by nearly a hundred enemy fighters. The bomber shot down seven fighters, probably destroyed two more, damaged an undetermined number, and flew home with the unscathed crew in buoyant spirits.

The ground crews made continuous changes and modifications to the airplanes, increasing power and speed and generally improving performance. Nothing could have proved better the stability of the great airplane than the flight of Captain Charles Joyce; at 10,000 feet all four engines quit when his tanks ran dry. Undaunted, Joyce flew his plane down without power and came in for a perfect dead stick landing.

Over the Singapore naval base, Lieutenant Jack T. Hull, bombardier of the B-29 *Pioneer III*, wrote one of the bloodiest and most heroic of Twentieth Bomber Command pages. As the B-29 moved in for its bombing run, enemy fire tore open Hull's face, destroyed his left eye, and severely injured his right hand and arm.

Hull slapped an oxygen mask to his face, stayed at his bombsights without informing the crew of his injuries, and salvoed his bombs on signal from the lead airplane. He then closed the bomb-bay doors and the rack switches, and remained at his station so that he would not disturb the crew until the formation swung away from its bombing run. Only then did he call for help.

Lieutenant Mills Bales recounted an attack over the Gulf of Martaban: "A 20-mm. shell exploded in the cockpit, severing our hydraulic lines and turning everything into a mass of flames. The Jap kept riddling us. One engine failed, and with most of the plane ablaze, we went into a steep spiral, dropping from 24,000 to 12,000 feet within three minutes. Then another reconnaissance B-29 came along and chased off the fighter.

"The pilot, Captain James E. Lyons, had severe burns on his hands and face, and was glassy-eyed and in a bad state of shock. The flight engineer, Lieutenant Frank Thorpe, had deep burns on his hands, and my hands and nose were blistered. Worst of all was the bombardier, Lieutenant William Kintis. All of his clothes were burned off, and he was a very terrible sight.

"Lyons and Thorpe managed to extinguish the cockpit fire and salvo the bomb-bay tanks with much difficulty. The men in the rear completely stripped the plane, but it still seemed too badly crippled to fly far.

"We talked it over and agreed that ditching would be certain death because the likelihood that the plane would explode upon contact with the water. If we bailed out, it was unlikely that the bombardier could survive.

"Kintis, who was in agony, heard us and said, "Listen, if you're going to risk your lives to try to save me, let's get out of here.'

"Less than a minute after the last man hit the silk, the plane exploded. The other B-29 circled a couple of times, tossed out a life raft, and then had to leave because its fuel supply was getting short.

"I was in the water about twenty hours with a leaking

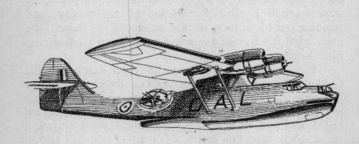

British PBY

Mae West, and fought off some sharks with a shoe. I was astonished and delighted to see a British PBY taxiing toward me. It also rescued Captain Lyons, Lieutenant Thorpe, and two enlisted men, and few us to Calcutta. A British submarine picked up four of the others. Lieutenant Kintis and two of the gunners were never found. . . ."

EXIT MATTERHORN

After ten months of combat operations, Project Matterhorn, the plan for attacking the Japanese home islands from bases on the Asian mainland, came to a halt. How successful was the campaign? Any exact evaluation is impossible to make, but a statement in the *Official History of the A.A.F. in World War II* will suffice: " . . . the strategic results of VHB [Very Heavy Bomber] operations from Chengtu were not a decisive factor in the Japanese surrender."

The U.S. Strategic Bombing Survey reported that the results of Matterhorn "did not warrant the diversion of effort entailed; the aviation gasoline and supplies used by the B-29's might have been more profitably allocated to an expansion of the tactical and antishipping operations of the Fourteenth Air Force in China."

That the Asian-based B-29 strikes were of questionable value could not be denied; harsh critics of the entire project condemned Matterhorn as being ill-advised and exorbitant in cost.

Twentieth Bomber Command carried out forty-nine B-29 missions in its ten active months of life, flew a total of 3,058 sorties, and dropped 11,477 tons of high-explosive and incendiary bombs. More to the point—only a small fraction of this effort was hurled at the industrial targets of Japan proper.

In sum: No matter what its successes, or to what extent we may qualify the criticisms, the Twentieth Bomber Command operations that introduced the B-29 to combat can only be regarded as a failure.

The official title for Matterhorn was "Early Sustained Bombing of Japan."

"The bombing was neither early nor sustained," reads

an official A.A.F. report. "It achieved no significant results, and whatever intangible effects were produced were obtained at too dear a price."

But Matterhorn was only one phase of the mounting tide against Japan. The invasion of Saipan on June 15th meant graduation day for the B-29's—adequate bases and a strong, sustained supply system. That was all they needed.

4

ISLAND INVASION

The GI's told a story about an American who trapped a Japanese soldier in a cave and demanded: "Come out and surrender!" In perfect English the Japanese screamed: "Come and get me, you souvenir-hunting sonuvabitch!"

There are many statistics that were used in early 1944 to describe the island of Saipan, in the Marianas. From the viewpoint of the Army Air Forces, two statistics were more important than any others. The first was that Saipan was an island of approximately seventy-five square miles, making it ideal for airfields that could hold fleets of B-29 bombers. The second statistic was even more important: Saipan was 800 miles closer to Tokyo than Chengtu or Chungking on the Chinese mainland.

When Marquis Koichi Kido, Lord Keeper of the Privy Seal of the Imperial Japanese Government, was asked by our interrogators at what point of the war he considered that Japan was lost, he replied: "It was rather early—after the fall of Saipan. It was my opinion at that time that it was advisable to give consideration to discontinuing the war. First, the fall of Saipan meant the intensification of American air attacks upon the Japanese home islands. Second, it revealed the failure of the navy, upon which our Japanese people in general had placed a great deal of reliance. . . . "

More than a few Japanese shared these thoughts. Indeed, so violent was the reaction of the Japanese hierarchy to what was considered the worst debacle of the war, that

47

the cabinet of Hideki Tojo (which had ruled with a steel fist for many years) was forced to resign.

Saipan is one of the islands of the Marianas chain that stretches in a long, curving line for almost 500 miles, from tiny Farallon de Pajaros on its northern tip to Guam at the southern end. Air-power strategists were interested only in the three largest southern islands for the B-29's—Saipan, Tinian, and Guam.

Saipan is a mountainous island; Mount Tapotchau rises to 1,554 feet. This peak, and other slopes on the island, were infested with hundreds of artillery and mortar pieces. And Mount Tapotchau wasn't just a gently rising slope; it had razored edges, it was honeycombed with caves, and it was murder to take.

Around this major defensive point—from which the Japanese poured heavy fire into our forces, and saw every move the Marines made—is high terrain, very rugged, with steep cliffs and deep ravines. On the west coast, where the assault forces hit the beaches, is Lake Susupe. The gullies and ravines were bad enough; this area was worse—for it was a large and almost impenetrable swamp. The rest of the island wasn't much better—pines, willows, sword grass, and tangled ground vines.

In the first two weeks of fighting, the Marines and Army troops suffered *three times as many casualties as were sustained at Tarawa.* In fourteen days we lost 1,474 men killed, 878 missing (the Japanese weren't taking any prisoners), and 7,400 wounded. Another way to judge the cost: Saipan in those first two weeks cost one-fourth of all our casualties in the massive landings in Normandy.

The battle for the Marianas cost the Japanese more than 43,000 men. More than half of these troops were on Saipan—and almost to the last man they had to be killed.

The 2nd and 4th Marine Divisions hit the beaches on the morning of June 15th. "The Japs didn't have much in the way of beach defenses," a Marine said later. "There really weren't any defense lines. They counted pretty much on what they had in the way of firepower in the mountains, all those guns that were dug in. When the first wave of the amphibious tractors passed over the outlying reef, about a thousand yards offshore, they began to open up."

Fortunately, this initial fire was not so dense as to interfere seriously with the ship-to-shore movement; within twenty minutes after the first wave hit the beach 8,000 Marines were ashore. But at this stage of the landings "things just went haywire." Many of the amphibious tractors failed to push ahead of the beachhead line; instead, they unloaded the troops near the water's edge. The result was chaos—"untold confusion and congestion," in the terms of the official survey of the operation.

The tactical situation caused the 2nd Marine Division, through no fault of its own, to land nearly a half-mile north of its assigned beaches, and the hapless Marines soon were forced to fight for their lives in two directions—to the south as well as east. Because of this error, the two Marine divisions lost contact with each other, and it took four days of fierce, bloody fighting to close the dangerous gap in their lines. The Japanese fought with fanatical heroism, and the Marines were soon faced with casualties beyond all expectations. Only by their own unremitting drive and willingness to come to grips with the powerful defenders did they establish on the first day a front of some five miles across, with a depth averaging 1,500 yards.

It was still a situation that could be described as "fluid." The Japanese retained possession of the hills overlooking the beach and poured in heavy fire—a prelude to Iwo Jima. A front depth of 1,500 yards is not at all healthy, and the Marines faced serious dangers of infiltration and counterattack.

The next morning their worst fears were confirmed. Well-organized and brilliantly led counterattacks slashed into both Marine forces. The attacks were repulsed, but the invasion forces were left with severe losses, seriously weakening their position. The Marines held their precious ground and waited for supplies and reinforcements to move ashore. Not until late afternoon of the second day of the attack were they able to drive toward a line that could protect the beachhead.

To make up for the heavy Marine losses and to increase our strength against the intensive Japanese resistance, the Marine Commander (General Holland Smith) ordered the Army's 27th Infantry Division, waiting on ships off Saipan, into the attack against Aslito Airfield. Two battalions of the 165th Regimental Combat Team were the first units to come ashore.

It was during the second week of the battle that both the Marines and Army troops ran into the fiercest fighting of the effort to take the island. Corporal Charles Buydos of the 165th Combat Team, who came ashore at Green Beach with a group of 105-mm. howitzers, recalls the events at the time:

105-mm Howitzer

"This was the period when everyone had some tough slugging. To our left the Marines were given a really bloody job—they had to scale the cliffs and ravines of Mount Tapotchau, and the Japs were dug in solidly. It was a savage, close-quarters fight for those gyrenes. On our right, facing somewhat lighter resistance, were more Marines who moved out against the Kagman Peninsula. We were in the center, moving down a valley. It was rough, no question about that."

What Buydos didn't add was that the Army forces—

his 165th Combat Team, and the 105th Infantry—were bucking what official Marine documents call "one of the best fortified pieces of land on the island." The Army troops soon gave it a title that was all too well deserved—Death Valley. The soldiers faced two defensive lines of caves and strong points, paralleling each other. These two lines, in turn, ran parallel to the planned line of advance. Because the Japanese were able to pour a withering stream of fire at the exposed Army troops, rapid movement was made impossible.

If this wasn't bad enough, to the left the route to be followed by the soldiers led almost directly beneath the almost vertical cliffs of the Tapotchau Rang. And directly to the right was a high, thickly-wooded ridge that the Army and Marine foot soldiers quickly named Purple Heart Ridge.

The fighting during successive days became a nightmare of slugging it out with the desperate Japanese, and the individual pockets of resistance, manned with die-to-the-last-man defenders, often slowed the advance of the combined forces. Saipan soon became a battle measured in weeks; but by July 7th the end appeared to be in sight.

That, however, was the morning on which Lieutenant General Yoshio Saito, the ranking Japanese army commander, went all out to kill as many Americans as possible. He ordered a final banzai charge at our lines.

Four thousand fanatical, screaming soldiers, each man sworn to "take seven lives to repay our country," charged the Marine and Army troops. They carried everything from machine guns to knives and bayonets tied to the end of long bamboo poles, and they stormed the battle-weary GI's with a howling fury.

The 105th Combat Team of the 27th Division, ill-disposed to meet the furious wave of Japanese, took the brunt of the attack. Between the First and Third Battalions was a gap of 300 yards, and a breakthrough was quickly accomplished by the whirlwind of shrieking, yelling Japanese soldiers who had no fear of dying—only that they might fail to take their toll of "seven lives" for every Japanese lost.

General Saito's troops stormed through the Army soldiers, hurled them back, and finally surrounded the surviving remnants of the regiment with their backs to the sea. More than a mile to the rear of the front were two full batteries of Marine artillery, and the churning wave of fanatical Japanese reached these batteries and quickly overran the Marines.

By dark, the 106th Infantry had followed through with a pounding counterattack, recovered the artillery positions, and occupied just about half of the lost ground. Units of the 105th Infantry, however, remained isolated during the night, and fought off Japanese who infiltrated their lines to attack with knives and bayonets.

On July 8th all units of the 27th Division, except the 165th, which was attached to the Second Marine Division, were relieved by the Marines. On July 9th it was just about over—hundreds of Japanese soldiers and civilians, preferring death to capture, leaped from the cliffs of Marpi Point to rocky shoals far below. For weeks afterward the Marines mopped up caves and blasted pillboxes manned by diehard defenders. But July 9th—nearly four weeks after the Marines poured ashore—was the end of all organized resistance.

Three and one half months later—on November 24th, 1944—one hundred B-29 bombers took off from Saipan to launch the first heavy-bomber attack against the city of Tokyo.

5

BUILDUP ON SAIPAN

The history of B-29 operations from the Marianas in the Pacific can be dated from the arrival of the first air-service groups that moved in two months before the bombers arrived, built roads out of crushed coral, hauled supplies, set up maintenance equipment on the line, all *"to be ready for the coming of the first B-29."*

The story of how thousands of men prepared for the coming of the first B-29 to Saipan is an epochal tale all in itself. And it is in this area more than any other that we find the stark difference between heavy-bomber operations against Japan proper, and those from England against Germany. Here there existed no roads or factories, no supply depots or deep harbors, no rail lines or ammo dumps or spare-parts fields, no abundance of emergency fields to fly to—in short, everything our heavy bomber operations enjoyed in Europe was lacking in the Marianas. It was a problem of starting absolutely from scratch, relying upon the Navy as a combined highway, shipping, railroad, and port facility—all right in Japan's frontyard.

The building of the longest runways in the Pacific was a job that the best engineers in the Pentagon said flatly "couldn't be done." The Japanese propagandists from Tokyo who lashed out at the American forces on Saipan ridiculed the engineers.

And for a while it looked as if they were right. Except that the Aviation Engineers—the 804th, 805th, 806th, 1878th and 1849th Engineer Aviation battalions—who called themselves the Flying Castles, hadn't read the book that proved it was all impossible. Six days after the invasion of the island of Saipan, they poured ashore with their tools and equipment. Even as stray bullets and shells crashed into their work areas, they had filled in 600 craters on Aslito Strip to make it usable for fighters and bombers. Then they added a thousand feet to the strip (which became known as Isley Field), and spun around to begin work on the new heavy-bomber runways and hardstands.

They worked day and night, literally on a continuous twenty-four-hour-a-day basis. During July and August the men were almost driven mad by violent tropical storms. To get the tons of coral they needed for construction, the men put together an army of bulldozers and literally chewed down two coral mountains! A procession of more than one hundred four-ton trucks carried away coral shavings to provide surfacing for runways, hardstands, and roads. And, of course, there were Japanese fighters and bombers to contend with, staging from Iwo Jima, bombing and strafing the construction teams.

Some of the construction jobs were epics. The Negro engineers of the 1849th Battalion, for example, built the hard-surfaced, three-lane, three-mile highway from the coral pits to the runways in exactly five day and nights. Indicative of the value of this job was that the time required for the trucks to transport the coral to the construction site of the airfields dropped from five hours of tortuous bumps to fifteen minutes of fast, smooth driving.

Another problem was producing the liquid asphalt that was to be used as a final surfacing. Engineers in England would have screamed had they seen the job as it was done on Saipan. The problem was so serious that the experts in Washington warned the A.A.F. that "black top couldn't be used in the Marianas," because liquid asphalt cannot be shipped. The engineers asked that hard asphalt be shipped to Saipan in drums, and they would take over from there. An ingenious "home-made" melting plant was rigged up by the engineers out of a boiler from a former Japanese sugar plant; then they built a smokestack from welded oil drums. They rushed the "plant" into operation, and soon were producing seven hundred tons of asphalt daily. Tied in with the

2,000 tons per day capacity of the coral quarry, Saipan began to change in a hurry.

Getting the runways built was considered so critical a priority job that not even the general's jeep was allowed to travel around the island without carrying coral. The two giant B-29 fields were needed immediately, and the engineers had to make each Superfortress strip 200 feet wide and 8,500 feet long. They also pounded out six miles of taxiways and some 200 hardstands for parking the great bombers. The engineer battalions also built Kobler and Kagman Point fields nearby, from which B-24 and other bombers and fighters operated. They hacked out a system of roads (which were so busy that traffic signals were installed), erected a 40,000-gallon gas storage depot, and facilities to support all the rest of the work.

Unfortunately, the construction job didn't move as quickly as had been planned. Japanese resistance was much more severe than had been anticipated, and this slowed down operations. The conditions under which the engineers worked were not conducive to rapid construction, and their particular problems delayed completion of the projected work.

General Hansell had been informed, on his way to Saipan with the first B-29, that he would find four giant B-29 fields nearing completion when he arrived at Saipan. But by October 12th this wasn't the case; there were only two partially completed fields. And there weren't any repair shops, camps, or housing facilities. "Ground echelons of our bombardment groups," the general recalled, "had been put ashore and told by the island commander, 'There's a pretty good place under the bluff—go and build yourselves a camp.' Most of the men were mechanics, not trained for construction work. But they went ahead and built quite a good camp."

Normal procedures would have been for the construction engineers to have built living quarters first, but Saipan didn't exactly call for normal procedures. The officers and men who were to support B-29 operations dug in to erect their own tents, mess halls, offices, showers and latrines. They worked right around the clock as did the engineers who hammered away at the job of the runways and hard-stands, working at night under batteries of floodlights, and "to hell with the goddamned Japs." One naval observer looked at the frenzied activity and said that it looked like Henry Kaiser had taken over the island.

The 6th Naval Construction Brigade, with all construction forces under the Seabee commander, started to reshape the island of Tinian as a B-29 base. Several giant strips were built, and it was on Tinian's North Field that the 509th Composite Group—the unit that carried the atomic bombs to Japan—was based. After construction had proceeded for several months, two heavy bomb wings moved onto the island.

By November of 1944 construction was under way on Guam's North Field. Here all major construction forces, both Army and Navy, worked together under the 5th Naval Construction Brigade. This did not lead to the smoothest of working relationships, for the Navy viewed Guam as a major forward base for strikes against Formosa and other targets, and relegated the B-29 program to the lowest possible priority. After harbor development, headquarters buildings, supply facilities, medical facilities, came development of aviation facilities. To put it mildly, the A.A.F. and the Navy engaged in rather heated discussions on the matter. General Curtis LeMay openly condemned the Navy's grudging logistical support that put his air bases "91st on a list of priorities, below . . . fleet recreation [and] tennis courts."

The exact details of logistical support were *never* worked out in fine print, and until the very day that the war ended there were heated arguments under way. The student of logistical operations in the British Isles may find interest in the knowledge that the XXI Bomber Command fought an intensive air war against Japan without an air service command, without its own aviation engineer battalions, without control of an air depot, without ordnance companies, lacking in any major support facilities, without hangars or extensive maintenance shops, under enemy fire, exposed to torrential tropical storms, and with the barest minimum of work and service troops.

Unable to function without close naval logistical cooperation, the B-29's had to turn to the Navy for shipping, construction, and the maintenance of its airfields; in the same breath, the B-29 commanders were dependent upon Army supply systems for all basic and technical supplies, and for depot support.

Under these conditions it is understandable, perhaps, that the *Official History of the A.A.F. in World War II* describes the logistical avenues as "circuitous, cumbersome, and confusing," and a system of which "few people fully understood their labyrinthine ramifications."

The number of aircraft in the theater, operating from the small islands, was almost beyond belief. In August 1944 there were 999 planes of all types; eleven months later there were more than 3,000 aircraft on hand, and the profusion was bewildering. More important—as late as October of 1944 there were no B-29's in the Marianas; in mid-July of 1945 nearly a thousand of the great raiders were actively on hand, and this does not include the number of planes that were lost in battle and because of operational or mechanical reasons.

Indeed, the B-29's poured into the combat theater so rapidly that the replacements of combat crews fell behind the supply of aircraft. By the war's end a total of 1,437 B-29 bombers, and 42 F-13's (B-29's converted to reconnaissance planes) were in the Marianas or on Iwo Jima. The total number of crews came to but 1,892—and this was so slim a margin under intensified operations that the shortage of combat crews finally became the most limiting factor of B-29 combat operations.

BOOMTOWN: AMERICANIZING THE MARIANAS

From the very beginning, a pattern of living began to take form, repeated with minor variations, on the three islands—Saipan, Guam, and Tinian. The Age of the Bulldozer was born, and it was with this clanking, snorting, treaded monster that the GI's shoved ignominiously aside the battered remnants of Japanese occupation. The bulldozer was miraculous in its ability to change the earth itself, but sometimes it drove the men to distraction. Seabees and aviation engineers pitched their puptents in the morning near a hill or some clump of trees for a landmark, and at nightfall they couldn't find their way home. The trees or even the entire hill was gone, victim to the snorting, bleating 'dozers. In just a few hours the sharpbladed mechanical monsters would uproot acres of jungle, and hack out the beginnings of an airfield.

Saipan changed overnight. Once it looked like a tropical paradise on a cheaply tinted postcard—lush vegetation, hills, the sea just beyond the beaches. In no time at all it looked like a scene out of the old west—a pioneer settlement that could have been any gold-rush town.

"The winter of 1944-1945 was a season of mud or dust. When the ground echelons of the 314th Bomb Group arrived at Guam on 18 January," wrote one of the editors of *Impact*, "they hacked a site out of the jungle, and in the evenings drove eight miles to Harmon Field for a shower, and were dust-covered again by the time they got home. Men working on the runway at North Field set up their cots on the sidelines and rigged up puptents on top of the cots. On more than one morning they woke up after a heavy rain to find that the water around them was cot high, and the puptents presented the rather miraculous appearance of being pitched on the surface of a lake."

There were still plenty of Japanese around. Most were furtive, holed up in caves and grottos. On Saipan, however, they were more than a nuisance; here there were groups that still followed leaders and worked under some form of organization.

There were hundreds, perhaps even a few thousand of them still around. They lurked in the thick foliage and behind rocks and in the caves on Topatchau. They holed up in abandoned tanks and shattered pillboxes, they dug holes in the jungle floor and hid in daylight. Every now and then they would say good-by to the few women they'd dragged into the hills with them, come out of their holes, and prepare for a final act of derring-do that would have satisfied the Emperor personally.

The 314th Wing had its own private banshee, a Japanese soldier who was probably insane, but who possessed powerful lungs. About three o'clock in the morning he

P-47 Thunderbolt

would ease his way soundlessly from the jungle to the camp, hide in the brush, and howl hideously. He sounded like a soprano wolf screeching at the moon. It was not at all restful.

One of the Wing's air-service groups, which had pitched its camp on the edge of the jungle, was so un-nerved by the sights and sounds of prowling Japanese that at night they arranged their vehicles in a big semicircle and directed all their headlights into the wilderness. The Japanese laughed at them and threw stones at the headlights.

Not all of it was laughable, for some of the toughest fighting men the Japanese had in their Army had been left behind, and they never thought of quitting. They killed marines and soldiers who strayed far from their camps and ventured into the jungle. They came out of the hills at night, stealing clothing and food from the kitchens. They had regular water holes where they gathered their drinking water.

Every now and then the GI's got fed up with it and went out into the hills. One group set an ambush, and waited patiently until several Japanese had shown themselves. Then they opened fire. They killed all the Japanese in sight, and those that had not revealed themselves fled wildly—only to run into a second group of GI's who cut them to pieces. That little excursion by itself killed more than sixty Japanese troops.

But until the end of the war—and for some time afterward—it just wasn't safe to wander at night. Forms rose up out of the darkness, struck expertly with knives or bayonets, and vanished, leaving behind a dead or bloody GI. Long after the war, these Japanese were still convinced that the island would be retaken.

One Japanese—he must have been an officer because he carried a sword—killed four men before the GI's finally trapped him. He had a trademark—he killed by slicing in with the sword at the leg near the groin, and then spun the sword up and around with a curving, slashing motion, disemboweling his victim. When the GI's finally caught him—first stunning him with concussion grenades set off by a wire across the jungle path—they didn't leave very much to bury.

The real problem was the Japanese who did their best to interfere with the bombing operations. Their trick was to load their bodies with high explosives, hide in the underbrush alongside the runway, and then dash out, hoping to hurl themselves at a B-29 or another airplane, thus killing as many Americans as possible and destroying the airplane. They were impossible to capture alive—if they were surrounded by troops, they yanked the pin on a grenade, cupped it beneath their chins, and blew themselves to pieces.

Much worse than the Japanese soldiers still hiding out were the rats. They were rampant. Once a big de-ratting contest was held by the residents of several Quonsets on Saipan. For every rat shot dead, a rat was painted above the front door. For every wounded rat that got away, half a rat was painted up, and listed as a "probable." At the end of the two weeks the men in the winning Quonset were given a beer party by the losers. It was a wonderful system—everybody got to fire their guns, they killed rats, and then ended up getting drunk.

"By April," wrote an officer, "Guam's Route No. 1 became what is practically the symbol of America: a straight paved road, lined with telephone poles, and jammed with traffic. You felt that such a highway must lead to a big city. The road had other plans. Riding northward on Route No. 1, you came to a rise, and then suddenly it was spread out before you: North Field with its two 8,500-foot runways, its miles of taxi strips and hardstands, covered by a sea of B-29's, their rows of wings shining in the sun, their tail fins arching up like surf. It was a satisfying way for one highway to end—and another to begin."

FINAL CALLING CARDS

"There are Jap raids galore," one officer wrote home. "Those babies aren't fooling. Ever since the first Tokyo raid they have come over night after night, and despite the great numbers of planes we shoot down, they manage to get in their damage and keep everyone on the alert. It's getting so everyone screams at the slightest noise, and we really have built some sturdy foxholes."

On November 2nd, nine twin-engined Japanese bombers came in to the deck to strike at Isley and Kobler Fields. The enemy did little damage, and lost three of his bombers. Five days later there were two separate attacks of five planes each; again the Japanese left three bombers behind them without achieving damage to any of the big American bombers. Then came the first B-29 attack against Tokyo; it was the same as kicking a hornet's nest as far as the Marianas bases were concerned.

It was still dark the morning of November 27th when two Mitsubishi twin-engined raiders streaked in over the water and caught the B-29's as they were loading up for another raid. The two Japanese planes hit hard and accurately. Before they swung out to sea they left three B-29's flaming; one exploded and showered other planes with molten metal. That day twenty bombers which had been scheduled to be over Tokyo remained at the base for repairs, or were completely beyond salvaging.

At noon of the same day, fourteen Zero fighters repeated the low-level attack, slipping through the defensive radar screen. Fortunately, most of the B-29's were gone—in fact, they were then over Tokyo—for the Zeros had a field day of it, sweeping back and forth for a half hour over Saipan. Japanese gunnery was sharp; the Zero pilots set three B-29's aflame (they were destroyed completely) and damaged two others.

Saipan struck back with some effect; anti-aircraft gunners shot down six of the Zero fighters, but came in for a bitter lashing when they also—inexcusably—blew a P-47 Thunderbolt out of the sky. The fighters shot down four Zeros.

It was the last daylight attack against Saipan, but the Japanese were persistent, and came in at night. Several raids were ineffective, but on December 7th the Japanese got smart, teamed up for a combined strike simultaneously from low and high altitude. They destroyed three of the big bombers and damaged another twenty-three.

Christmas of 1944 was the last of the Japanese attacks, for by now Iwo Jima—the island on which the Japanese staged their raids—was being ground into a pulp by continuing heavy strikes by our bombers and carrier planes. On their final stab of any effectiveness at Saipan, the combined high-low attack destroyed one B-29, smashed three more beyond repair, and damaged yet another eleven.

The defenders were caught flat-footed. The Japanese spilled chaff (aluminum foil) into the air to blanket the radar defenses and the fighters came screaming in out of the dark, guns blazing, while the floodlights were still on the airfields. One B-29 was loaded with 8,000 gallons of gasoline, and a mixture of three tons of high explosives and incendiaries; it was parked alongside a gasoline trailer holding another 2,200 gallons of fuel. Both blew up on Isley Field with a glare that illuminated the entire island.

"The engineers jumped into the breach," related General Hansell, "and they did one of the finest jobs I have ever seen. Although the Jap Bettys were dropping many small anti-personnel bombs and there was quite a bit of confusion, they brought up their heavy equipment, rode right at the exploding fiery wreckage, piled the burning B-29's into big heaps with their bulldozers, brought up dirt and threw it on top, and then drove over the whole mess to squash the fire out. Their action saved many planes from destruction."

Betty

And that was the end of it. The Japanese attacks did not interfere seriously with the heavy-bomber operations, but they were an expensive and lethal nuisance. In their attacks the Japanese sortied eighty fighters and bombers over Saipan and Tinian; they lost about half of this number. But for the cost of forty planes they destroyed eleven of the great B-29's (a fair exchange to them), inflicted heavy damage to another eight, and minor damage to thirty-five. In so doing, they killed forty-five men and wounded another two hundred.

For the Japanese, however, time was running out fast.

6

THE ATTACKS BEGIN

First the B-29's tried their wings and gingerly flexed their muscles. The crews that arrived at Saipan were well trained in the operation of their aircraft, but they lacked the time in the United States to fly extensively in unit formation. To prepare for the strikes against Japan, the XXI Bomber Command decided on several "shakedown" missions to be flown against Truk and Iwo Jima. The skies over Japan weren't exactly suitable for working out the fine details of formations, timing, and the thousand and one things that make up an effective attacking force. Thus the crews were informed that they would undergo an extensive course in theater indoctrination, formation flying, rendezvous, communications, over combat targets that were "less vigorously defended" than those on the main islands of Japan.

On October 28th the first strike was made against Dublon Island in the Truk group. The attack included overwater flying, a demand for excellent navigation, moderately light Japanese defenses—and would serve to keep the once-mighty bastion neutralized; Truk had borne the incessant attacks of Seventh Air Force B-24 Liberators for many months. The constant pounding from the air kept the Japanese off balance, prevented any power buildup, and eliminated the need for a costly and time-consuming invasion of the island group.

Eighteen Superfortresses participated in the attack, each airplane carrying three tons of high-explosive bombs.

64

Four B-29's suffered mechanical failure and aborted. The remaining fourteen bombed the Dublon submarine pens from 25,000 feet. About forty per cent of the bombs struck the target area, but since this was a training mission General Hansell was well satisfied. The Japanese cooperated by throwing up some flak and scrambling a single Zero whose pilot watched everything with interest but remained circumspectly far away from the bristling B-29's.

Two days later eighteen bombers went out again; the Japanese reacted in the same manner, but the bombing left much to be desired. The third attack, on November 2nd, made it all too obvious that the crews still had much to learn about using the B-29 effectively. The bomb dispersal was described as "terrible," and defied all attempts to draw a bomb plot.

Zero Fighter

After Truk came three practice strikes against Iwo Jima. For the green B-29 crews this represented a step up the ladder. Seven hundred and twenty-five miles to the north of Saipan, Iwo had plenty of flak, a belligerent garrison, and enough Zero fighters to make things hot. During the three attacks the Japanese defenses remained somewhat subdued, except for one occasion when several Zeros raced in. One managed to flip a phosphorous bomb onto a Superfortress, inflicting the first damage on any bomber of the XXI Bomber Command.

In subsequent months, the Command employed Truk as a regular training course. Until the end of the war, the crews ran up a total of thirty-two strikes against the atoll. It was perfect for the practice of the new crews; there were forty AA guns and some old beat-up fighters, but none of these could really harm the great bombers as they cruised five and six miles high. To the complete astonishment of A.A.F. interrogators, Japanese officers at Truk after the war rated the B-29 bombing as "excellent."

THE RECON FLIGHTS

Certain targets in Japan were obvious—Tokyo, for example, was a natural choice. Not only a prime military target, Tokyo headed the list also as a psychological target. An effective strike against the capital, the home of the Emperor and the center of the Japanese war machine, would have enormous repercussions among the population—to say nothing of the B-29 crews, the people back in the states, and our Allies everywhere.

No matter what the value of other targets, none were so appealing to the strategic planners of the XXI Bomber Command—and the staff of the Twentieth Air Force, with headquarters in the Pentagon—as the Japanese aircraft industry. It was an industrial complex of the utmost value to the Japanese, and it was also vulnerable to the B-29's.

It should be emphasized that at this time all planes still carried high-explosive bombs. The concept of burning Japan out of the war had appealed to many, but at this stage the Japanese strikes followed closely the methods employed in Europe with the Eighth Bomber Command—high-altitude precision bombing.

In 1944 Japanese industry produced 28,180 airplanes, the majority of them combat types of improved performance. A few giant combines—Mitsubishi, Nakajima, Kawasaki, and Tachikawa—produced more than two thirds of all Japanese aircraft. Mitsubishi, Nakajima, and Kawasaki alone turned out some 80 percent of all combat types. Because of the concentration of this industry in several cities—Tokyo, Nagoya, and Osaka—the system was extraordinarily vulnerable to attack.

Thus the XXI Bomber Command established as its primary mission the destruction of the Japanese aircraft- and engine-assembly plants, and then the major overhaul and repair facilities. This was the priority of attack:

Principal Engine Manufacturers:

    Mitsubishi Jukogyo, Nagoya Hatsudoki

    Nakajima Hikoki, Musashino Seisakusho

    Kawasaki Kokuki, Akashi

    Nakajima Hikoki, Tama Seisakusho

Principal Aircraft Component and Assembly Plants:

    Nakajima Hikoki, Ota Seisakusho, Takasaki area

    Kawasaki Kokuki, Kagamigahara, Nagoya area

    Nakajimi Hikoki, Koizumi Seisakusho, Takasaki area

    Mitsubishi Jukogyo Kokuki, Nagoya area

    Aichi Tokei Denki, Eitoku, Nagoya area

As secondary and last-resort targets, all of which were suitable for "blind bombing" through clouds by radar, the B-29's were given the port areas of Osaka, Nagoya, Tokyo, Kawasaki, Yokohama, Shimonoseki, Kure, Hiroshima, Kobe, Nagasaki, Sasebo, and Yokosuka; urban areas included Hiroshima, Kure, Niigata, Yawata, Tobata, Wakamatsu, Kurashiki, Kokura, Fukuoka, Nagasaki, Omuta, Moji, Kurume, and Nobeoka.

In addition to the precision attacks, the XXI Bomber Command was to undertake at least one major incendiary raid so that we could compare the effectiveness of this method with the precision strikes with high-explosive bombs.

Although the target selection appeared complete, the effectiveness of the operations to come was hindered seriously by a lack of detailed and accurate target intelligence. Photographic-reconnaissance B-29's flying from China had embarked on missions over Japan, but the bombers were at the maximum of their range, and left unphotographed the majority of targets that fell to the concern of the XXI Bomber Command.

On October 30th two F-13A (modified B-29's) reconnaissance planes arrived at Saipan after a two-stop, 33-hour flight from California. A short time later, one of the airplanes, piloted by Captain R. D. Steakley and named *Tokyo Rose* for her mission, droned at 32,000 feet over the Japanese capital. The weather was clear, and the cameras clicked away steadily. The airplane returned to Saipan with more than 7,000 invaluable prints that revealed long-hidden industrial secrets.

More of the F-13's went out, cruising high over all the Japanese targets. Despite intensive efforts the enemy managed to down only one of the probing Superfortresses—this on November 21st, over Nagoya. Before the first strike was launched against Tokyo, seventeen single-plane missions were flown over the Japanese home islands—nine for target selection and pinpoint, and eight missions for weather. The latter factor was to become one of the severest enemies of the B-29 campaign.

For some unexplained reason the Japanese were convinced that there were actually *two* B-29 reconnaissance planes over Tokyo on the first photographic mission. "At 1:30 P.M. on November 1st the first B-29's appeared over Tokyo," related Masatake Okumiya, officer in charge of naval aircraft assigned to the fighter defense of the home islands. "Aircraft spotters were astonished suddenly to discover the two huge planes on a reconnaissance mission high over the city. They dropped no bombs and left shortly after their arrival, but their appearance was a great shock to the military personnel charged with the mainland defense. Until these planes were sighted directly over the city, we had no idea that any airplanes were over Japan. Our patrol planes and ships had failed to sight the bombers and, despite the excellent flying weather, our interceptors could not catch the enemy planes. Within the next two weeks additional B-29's flew over Nagoya on reconnaissance missions, again with impunity. . . ."

WEATHER—THE CONSTANT ENEMY

Lieutenant General Millard F. Harmon, the Commanding General of Army Air Forces, Pacific Ocean Areas, understood the weather problems facing B-29 operations against Japan—and they were formidable. "Between Saipan and Tokyo," remarked General Harmon, "the weather is mostly bad. Nowhere else is there such turbulence, such unpredictable and sudden changes.

"Miles high over Tokyo, gales blow harder than any other place in the world, including Mt. Everest. *They reach a velocity of more than two hundred miles an hour.*

"This weather belt extends a thousand miles south of Tokyo. Always at some point it is violent. Our crews bombing Japan fly daily with the outside temperature at forty below zero."

General Harmon's words were more prophetic than even he realized. Several months later he himself was lost in unpredicted storm weather during a Pacific flight.

The heart of the weather problem was the severe frontal conditions which the B-29's would almost always have to encounter as they flew toward Tokyo. The weather systems were so bad that, as time was to prove, the B-29's were faced with scattered formations, severely increased fuel consumption when margins were too low to begin with, and navigation made so difficult that on occasions bombing crews missed landfall, and subsequently, their targets. If it happened on the way home, it could mean ditching in the open sea.

Even radar bombing left something to be desired, for combat proved quickly enough that the electronic systems, however marvelous, were a far cry from being the panacea for weather that the Pentagon believed. At extreme altitude the radar sets often malfunctioned. There had not been sufficient time to turn the radar operators into experts, and their own performance left something wanting. But what drove the crews mad were those winds of 200 miles per hour and even more. To fly directly into the wind was unthinkable not only in terms of fuel, but because it would have been suicide to move over Japan at a ground speed of only about 100 miles per hour. Flak and fighters would have had a field day.

And because of the extreme winds, bombing crosswind was also impossible. Drift simply couldn't be properly compensated for in the limited time available and under such severe conditions. To bomb downwind, the only alternative, meant streaking across Japan with a ground speed of 500 miles per hour and better. Under these conditions the limitations of both bombardiers and bombsights were exceeded. And then, the high winds made it impossible for a crew that had missed its target to come around again for a second try; sometimes the crew simply dumped the bombs into the sea, or hoped for a crack at a secondary target before running for home with a rapidly dwindling fuel supply.

Perhaps the best insight into the weather problem is provided in a report of December 1944 that came directly from the Marianas: "Forecasting the weather over Japan and along the 1,300-mile route from the Marianas to Japan is considered so important by the XXI Bomber Command that from its base on Saipan it schedules three 'Weather Strike Missions' daily. Primarily, these B-29 missions obtain weather data over Japan. Secondarily, bombs are dropped—just to make the trip even more worthwhile. The Japs call them 'nuisance raids.' Actually, they are much more than that. For this weather information helps to determine when and where the bulk of our bombs will fall.

"A long-term strategic bombing campaign requires, however, more than a day-by-day weather report. It requires a knowledge of the seasonal weather pattern that prevails generally over the entire area to be bombed.

" . . . in the winter, a flow of cold air sweeps down across the entire length of the Japanese island chain. Such an airflow results from the accumulation of a great mass of cold air over the icy interior of Siberia—an air mass whose principal escape route is toward the southeast across the main Japanese islands. This initially cold, dry air picks up considerable heat and moisture over the Sea of Japan. By the time it has reached the Japan coast, it yields cloud and precipitation on the windy northwestern slopes where it is lifted. Targets along this cloudy coast are not recommended for winter bombing.

"Then this far-traveling Siberian air, dried in its ascent over the mountain backbone of the islands, and warmed in its descent on the other side, arrives clear and dry over the plains that face the Pacific. Consequently, these areas are characterized by clear skies. This weather situation is particularly favorable for bombing the important target areas in the southeastern coastal plains of Honshu and Kyushu, including Tokyo and Nagoya.

"As this same cold air sweeps out across the Pacific toward Guam, it underruns warm, tropical air and produces the turbulent frontal area with towering clouds, the type that give pilots nightmares. Bombers flying from the Marianas to Tokyo must penetrate these fronts on their routes.

"While in winter there is a high probability of clear weather over targets near Tokyo, there is no certainty of it. A listing of weather conditions reported on the first eleven big-scale bombing missions to Tokyo and Nagoya, executed in the early winter, shows that weather problems exist even in this most propitious season.

24 Nov., Tokyo. No clouds to 9/10 undercast.

27 Nov., Tokyo. Jap mainland completely cloud-covered.

29 Nov., Tokyo. Solid undercast at target.

3 Dec., Tokyo. Clear with excellent visibility.

13 Dec., Nagoya. 1/10 cloud.

18 Dec., Nagoya. Three squadrons reported CAVU (Ceiling and Visibility Unlimited) directly over target. Six squadrons reported 8/10 to 10/10 cloud.

22 Dec., Nagoya. 6/10 to 10/10 cloud.

27 Dec., Tokyo. 1/10 cloud. Excellent visibility.

3 Jan., Nagoya. Primary target CAVU to 2/10 cloud.

9 Jan., Tokyo. Primary target CAVU.

14 Jan., Nagoya. Primary target 8/10 to 10/10 cloud.

"Strong winds and icing, typical of any high altitude winter flight, are reported frequently. On 3 December, for example, a 200-mile-an-hour wind swept over the target at an altitude of 29,000 to 31,000 feet. On another mission one B-29 landed home with only 80 gallons of gas, having used too much gas from the IP to the target because of winds. Also, its rear bomb bay doors would not close for three hours after bombing due to bad icing. Others reported severe icing in the astro-hatch after one hour's continuous flying at 30,000 feet, and the loss of 25 miles per hour due to rime icing.

"In the summer, the cloud cover shifts to the Pacific side of the Japanese islands, leaving a new set of targets exposed on the northwestern coast. Here the situation brings forth a weak flow of cool air circulating over the Sea of Japan. This air converges along the lower edge of the cloud air, with a strong flow of warm air from the Pacific. A sheet of clouds is then formed in the warm air as it ascends over the wedge of cold air. Where the warm air climbs the mountain backbone of Japan, clouds build up to great tights. These high clouds, and the rains that fall from them, are restricted to the southeastern side of the mountains, affording a protective summer blanket for such targets as Tokyo, while clear skies prevail on the northwest. Japan may be likened to a man in bed who pulls up the blanket to keep his ears hidden, only to expose his toes."

The walls of the bomber command offices on Saipan were covered with a profusion of maps and charts dotted with colored pins and flags. Multicolored tape streamers showed routes and distances; other symbols and pins identified clouds, winds, ships at sea, rescue planes, emergency radio frequencies, Japanese cities and anti-aircraft, fighter bases.

In mid-November of 1944, the pins finally concentrated in one area, and the multicolored tapes began to converge on Tokyo.

FIRST STRIKE

Everything was planned to get underway the morning of November 16th. The first attack against Tokyo was coded San Antonio I, and called for daylight bombing under visual conditions from 30,000 feet by eight B-29's. The target was the Musashino engine plant of the Naka-jima Company, about eleven miles northwest of the center of Tokyo. Here thirty thousand machinists produced more than 30 percent of all Japanese aircraft engines; it was a first-class target.

On the scheduled morning everything was all set to go—except the infamous Pacific weather. Isley Field on Saipan had been built in line with the prevailing winds that swept the Pacific. Normally, on Saipan, these came out of the east for six months, and then from the west for the re-mainder of the year. The night before the strike was to be flown, when every bomber was loaded with fuel and bombs, the wind died down altogether. And then the pre-vailing easterly wind shifted completely.

At Isley the runways sloped slightly down from west to east. This meant that the B-29's would have to take off on a long uphill pull. This is hazardous for a fully-loaded B-29 under any conditions, but then a torrential rain hit the field, and the term "hazardous" became akin to "suicide."

General Hansell: "About 4 A.M., as we were getting ready for the takeoff, we found to our horror that the wind had reversed itself and was coming from the west. Taxi-ways had been completed to the west but not to the east end. To taxi to the other end of the runway, involving a lapse of four to five minutes between takeoffs, would have run the assembly time beyond the available gasoline capac-ity. The wind was only 10 miles an hour, and we were loaded to 138,500 pounds. Reluctantly, we canceled the mission."

Twenty-four hours passed, and the hopes that had been buoyed suddenly sagged. As the second H-Hour ap-proached, a typhoon struck Saipan. Not only the camps and work areas, but the airstrips also were inundated with water. For five days the violent storm drifted slowly to-ward Tokyo, blocking the route of the B-29's, covering the "Hirohito Highway" with severe turbulence and high clouds. Bombers tracked the storm, reporting that it was too high to fly over and too wide to fly around.

The men bitched incessantly as the days passed, and called the B-29 "the best goddamned bomber that never left the ground." Then came November 24th—and the winds were right down the runway beneath a crystal-clear sky. This was *it*.

A long, thundering procession shook the island to its foundations; the great trembling roar created a strange form of dust storm. At exactly 15 minutes past six A.M. the first raider, *Dauntless Dotty*, started down the 8,500-foot runway. Loaded to its maximum with fuel and bombs, the gleaming, silver B-29 used every possible inch of the blacktop and some of the coral extension beyond the runway. Only then did it pull up slightly, just enough to bring up the gear. It sped out over the water, skimming the Pacific, and passed from sight.

At one-minute intervals, 110 of the Superfortresses followed *Dauntless Dotty* into the skies. Each airplane carried a maximum load of 8,070 gallons of fuel; aboard the entire formation was a total of 277.5 tons of bombs.

On the way in to Tokyo, seventeen B-29's aborted the first strike mission. Six airplanes were unable to attack their targets because of mechanical failures. The remaining eleven encountered heavy cloud cover (typhoon conditions still existed between Saipan and Iwo). Some formations, extending from 27,000 to 33,000 feet, were boosted along over Japan by a wind of 120 knots that gave them a ground speed of 445 miles per hour.

Over the target there was a thick undercast; only 24 planes struck the Musashino plant under visual conditions. Sixty-four B-29's smashed at dock and urban areas. Thirty-five of the airplanes that did bomb were forced to do so by radar.

About 125 Japanese fighters came up to battle with the B-29's—a bizarre mixture of Tojos, Zeros, Tonys, Nicks, Irvings, and a few unidentified types. The enemy pilots lacked the skill and tenacity of the Germans, and instead of coordinating their attacks, wandered in from all directions. Some were faint-hearted, others closed in to point-blank range, blasting away.

Only a single B-29 was lost. A Japanese pilot whose plane was set afire flew his burning Tony directly—deliber-

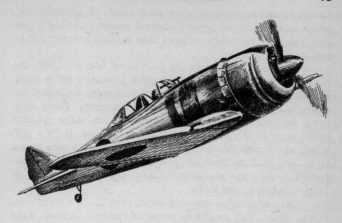

Tojo

ately—into the tail of a B-29. The Japanese fighter disinte-
grated, but the elevator and right horizontal stabilizer of
the B-29 were ripped away, and the airplane smashed into
the sea twenty miles off the Honshu coast, killing all
aboard.

On the way back, straggling through the storm area,
the B-29's were widely separated. Some landed at Guam
rather than Saipan because of congestion in the landing
pattern. One B-29 ran out of fuel and ditched at sea; air-sea
rescue saved the entire crew. All in all, it was quite a remarkable combat debut for unescorted bombers over so
great a range.

One B-29 lost in combat, another at sea. Eleven men
missing and presumed dead, one killed, four injured. Eight
B-29's were damaged from enemy fire; three from acci-
dental hits by B-29 guns.

In Musashino itself (as determined after the war), the
results were not as good as hoped for. But morale of the air
crews was at its highest—the XXI Bomber Command had
flown over 3,000 miles, had hit the toughest target area in
Japan, and had done so in extremely bad weather. No airplanes had been shot down; the one loss was by ramming.

Seven Japanese fighters were destroyed, 18 probably destroyed, and nine damaged—under a gunnery-claiming system that was "ten times tougher than we had it in the ETO," reported one gunner.

From this point on until the 9th of March, 1945, the XXI Bomber Command concentrated primarily on its high-altitude, daylight precision attacks that were delivered essentially against the Japanese aircraft factories. There were some deviations from this pattern—in the three months subsequent to the first attack from Saipan the B-29's also struck at the airfields on Iwo Jima, made a night area attack on Tokyo that terrified the people of the city, and experimented with some incendiary raids against urban areas of Tokyo, Nagoya, and Kobe.

Three days after the first attack, the B-29's were over Tokyo again. The results in terms of specific damage were disheartening; not a single bomb struck the Musashino engine plant, but 59 B-29's managed to dump 147 tons of bombs through an overcast on Tokyo.

The first night raid on Tokyo came with a mixture of high-explosive and incendiary bombs; 24 Superfortresses hit the city in three waves. Again the results left much to be desired; there were scattered burned-out patches covering an area barely one-tenth of a square mile.

On December 3rd, the B-29's were back—their fourth strike in only ten days against the Japanese capital. This in itself was an astonishing accomplishment, and it did not go unheeded by the Japanese, as well as by the men who planned the over-all B-29 attack program. Seventy of the big bombers hammered with barely improved results at Musashino, while other planes tossed their bombs into the Tokyo harbor facilities—this time with excellent precision because of the unexpected clear visibility. The Japanese were stiffening their resistance, and anti-aircraft fire for the first time was not only heavy, but dangerously accurate.

Six fighters went down to B-29 guns. One bomber lost a wing over the target and went down, spinning, in flames. After the war, when several members of the crew were freed from prison camps, it was learned that the airplane commander, Colonel Byron Brugge, had been beaten, tortured, and killed by his captors.

There was another suicide ramming, but this time the B-29, flown by Lt. D. J. Dufford, shook off the effects of the crash, and on three engines flew all the way back to Saipan. Four planes ditched on the way home.

The casualties from ditching were worse than from enemy action, a situation that would not be improved. The Navy worked beautifully to set up its air-sea rescue organization, but the majority of ditchings in the ocean were at night and in rough waters. Only some 25 per cent of these men were ever saved.

STEPPING UP THE PACE

The precision attacks hadn't brought about the results that were first anticipated by the strategic planners, but often the effects on the ground were far worse than were revealed to the intelligence officers who peered with worried frowns over the strike and reconnaissance photos. On December 13th, for example, the B-29 force came home somewhat battered after an attack on the Mitsubishi works in Nagoya. Fighters were out in force, Nagoya's famed (by now) anti-aircraft was brutal. Four B-29's went down to enemy action, another thirty-one were damaged—an unusually high number.

The strike photos showed that 16 per cent of all the bombs dropped by seventy planes over the target fell within a thousand feet of the aiming point, and that almost 20 per cent of the roofing area of the factory had been destroyed. But the pictures didn't tell the whole story, which was much worse for the Japanese who were on the receiving end.

Buildings were smashed heavily, valuable and irreplaceable machine tools destroyed; personnel losses came to 246 skilled workers killed and another 105 wounded. But what really counted was the dent in production—engine production fell from 1,600 new engines every month to 1,200, a severe loss to the Japanese, who were desperate for engines.

Masatake Okumiya, former Naval Commander and today a Major General of the Japanese Air Force, commented: "From late 1944 until early February of the following year the B-29's repeatedly attacked the aircraft factories in the Nagoya area in daylight raids, and on night missions bombed the civilian areas in Tokyo, Yokohama, Osaka, and Kobe. The B-29's made limited attacks against aircraft plants in the Kwanto and Kobe area. Our aircraft plants were to a dangerous degree smashed wreckage, for the high-explosive and incendiary bombs had shattered machinery, broken steel supports, burned out vast factory sections, and killed hundreds of workers.

"Mitsubishi's Nagoya aircraft and engine factories, Kawasaki's Akashi engine plant west of Kobe, and Nakajima's Ohta aircraft factory forty-five miles northwest of Tokyo all sustained great damage. Each of these factories were vital centers of airframe and engine production for both the Army and the Navy, and the B-29 attacks caused a drastic reduction in their production. . . . "

And, from the diary of the most famous aircraft engineer in all Japan, Jiro Horikoshi, who designed the Zero and other fighters, a report written after personally undergoing in the Mitsubishi plant one of the B-29 strikes: "This afternoon B-29's returned for their second attack against Nagoya, attacking the Mitsubishi Airframe Works, to which I belonged. As soon as the air-raid warning screamed we ran to a vacant lot near the main factory buildings and dropped into 'trenches' and 'dugouts' prepared as shelter areas. Protected against bomb shrapnel and blast, we searched for the bombers; we noticed several waves of B-29's, appearing white at a height I estimated to be thirty thousand feet. The great planes maintained a steady formation, releasing their bombs in salvos aimed to 'walk' across the factory buildings from the east to the west. This was my first experience under heavy air attack, and I remember vividly the screeching sound of the falling bombs and the unbelievable sound of the bomb explosions. My ears rang and I was deafened for hours afterward."

On December 22nd, under pressure from the Pentagon, the B-29's hit the home islands—Nagoya as the target—in a daylight incendiary mission. General Arnold's staff was firmly convinced that the Japanese cities were prime targets for incendiary raids, and he had been pressing for several test fire missions. Mass attacks had been planned for six selected cities, but there still existed strong arguments between those in favor of high-explosive precision attacks—the mainstay of A.A.F. bombing in Europe—and those who were striving for a mass fiery sweep of the Japanese city and factory areas.

Four days before the incendiary strike against Nagoya, the Twentieth Bomber Command had made its first attack against the military storage area of Hankow, China, using fire bombs. The results were spectacular, and the entire heart of the target area was completely gutted.

Although there was a pressing need for a full-scale incendiary attack to provide a basis for future strikes, the initial attempts were quite unsatisfactory. The December 22nd raid spread incendiary bombs by radar through a solid cloud undercast—the results in the Mitsubishi factory disrupted things but caused no losses in production.

There were additional attacks, most of them disappointing. A heavy mission on January 3rd, 1945, put 97 of the heavy bombers on their way to Nagoya with mixed incendiary and H.E. loads in the bays. But only 57 Superfortresses bombed the primary target.

The results were inconclusive, and the Japanese, despite the heavy fires started in scattered areas, considered the damage to be "slight." In the light of subsequent events, this was perhaps the most disastrous result that raid could have had, for on the basis of this rather ineffective mission they concluded that their fire-defense system was outstanding, and able to cope with any fires that might be started by the B-29's. Within a few short months that system literally drowned in fire.

There were some desultory raids, but on January 19th the silver bombers made a fantastic score. They struck at a target which until this time was undamaged by bombs—the vital Kawasaki factory about twelve miles west of Kobe. Here were the Akashi works, with some of Kawasaki's largest and most important factories, producing 17 per cent of all combat airframes and 12 per cent of all combat engines.

Sixty-two of the B-29's got through to the target, dumping 155 tons of bombs into the plants, and returning without loss to Saipan. The crews did not know it, but they had just turned in one of the most precise bombing strikes of the entire war, by any airplanes of any air force. *Every* important building, tool shop, and other facility in both airframe and engine departments was struck heavily, and most of them were smashed. *Production fell immediately by ninety per cent*! And the combine never returned to anything like its former production level.

SHIFT IN COMMAND

Strangely enough, this was the last mission to be ordered out by General Hansell. The day after the raid, Hansell turned over the reins of the XXI Bomber Command to Major General Curtis E. Le May, who was transferred to Saipan from a similar post with the XX Bomber Command on the Asian mainland.

The hard truth of the matter was that the B-29 strategic bombing campaign against the Japanese home islands simply wasn't paying off. The investment was fantastic, and the results weren't anything near worth the cost. In Washington, the pressure was being applied—the campaign was lagging, and no amount of juggling statistical data could hide the fact that the Japanese, although hurt, weren't being pushed that much more quickly to calling it quits.

Doubtless the Japanese would have been stunned to learn that the Pentagon was more than a little concerned over the "failure" of the B-29's to smash Japanese industry. From the viewpoint of the people in the factories and the cities, the B-29's were nothing less than a terrifying catastrophe. They could not imagine the destruction Washington visualized as within the capabilities of the new weapon.

General Hansell admitted readily enough to General Arnold in the Pentagon that the B-29 campaign had been deficient. He had, with remarkable and commendable candor, several times before evinced dissatisfaction with the performance of the B-29 forces under his command—yet he emphasized that compared to the B-29's operating from China, his 73rd Wing on Saipan had done a job that "doesn't look too bad."

Yet there were problems; that fact couldn't be avoided. The 73rd Wing had come to Saipan with a firm belief in the validity and effectiveness of bombing at night by radar; it was Hansell's unhappy task to change that belief into a trust in daylight precision attacks. The bombing accuracy of the B-29 crews was officially categorized as "deplorable," and this was perhaps the weakest of all the many links in the strategic bombardment campaign. The abortive rate was considered to be "shocking," averaging out to 21 per cent of all B-29's taking off for an attack. Too many planes were ditching in the open sea, and Washington was convinced that (1) this number could be reduced, and (2) air-sea rescue procedures could be improved to reduce the number of crews lost at sea.

To General Arnold, Hansell wrote that he too was at fault. Because of the pressing need to smash the Japanese aircraft industry, he had been driving his crews relentlessly. The excessive aborts and appalling losses at sea stemmed not from any faults or weakness in the men, Hansell stressed, but from inadequate maintenance and depot facilities.

There were other factors to consider—factors that extended the life of the Japanese targets and gave Japan a lease on combat and industrial strength they never realized was being afforded them. The entire B-29 campaign had been delayed by the fierce resistance on Saipan. But worst of all was the absolutely wretched and unexpected weather that crippled many strikes. So entangled was the logistical system and the manpower shortage that the planned buildup in the strength of the raids could not be achieved. The installations on Saipan, to say nothing of those expected on Tinian and Guam, were far behind original construction schedules.

All in all, the excuses were reasonable, but in Washington—where the A.A.F. and its leaders were coming under increasing fire—they weren't exactly palatable to the Joint Chiefs of Staff. A change, no matter how distasteful, was necessary. Hansell was out, and Le May in. Hansell was unexcelled in his ability to plan and organize. Le May had won no administrative laurels, but was already recognized for his hard-driving qualities. He was, in short, a trouble-shooter who had the reputation of getting things done.

He was also the worst thing that could have happened to the Japanese.

The first attacks under Le May showed no noticeable change in the pattern already established, but Le May was already studying target selection and had decided to mix his targets suddenly to throw off the Japanese defenses. Then, with the gentle prodding of Washington, he scheduled for his first mission in February an incendiary attack on the port and tightly packed industrial sections of Kobe. It was a major target—more than one million people, the sixth largest city in Japan, and by far its most important port. It included vital industries, which unhappily for the Japanese were jammed into an area so congested that they were prime for incendiary attack. In the area where the B-29's would strike with the incendiaries, more than 100,000 people were packed into a square mile.

There were so any aborts that of the 129 bombers that were airborne, only 69 managed to hit the city. Making their runs from 24,500 to 27,000 feet, and fighting off the determined attacks of some 200 fighters, they dumped 159.2 tons of incendiaries and 13.6 tons of fragmentation bombs into Kobe.

In the industrial southwestern district, more than a thousand buildings were either burned to the ground or seriously damaged. Nearly 5,000 people were rendered homeless—a small figure compared to later attacks. But what really counted was the effectiveness of the strike against local war production. Five major industries were severely hit. A major shipyard (one of two) cut all activities in half. Fabric and synthetic-rubber production was *completely wiped out*.

Precision attacks which followed this test incendiary strike left a pall of gloom in the intelligence sections—the bombers simply were not getting results. And the Japanese defenses were becoming so severe as to cause mounting worry at Saipan. In one raid of 84 B-29's, wild attacks by Japanese fighters added to heavy, accurate anti-aircraft fire shot twelve Superfortresses out of the sky and damaged another twenty-nine.

The more the B-29's experimented with incendiary raids, the more convinced Le May became that this was the answer. On February 25th the XXI Bomber Command put up its greatest effort to date. A total of 172 B-29's managed to get over Tokyo in a heavy wave, and dumped 453.7 tons of bombs into the city. A swarm of jellied-gasoline-magnesium bombs descended upon the city and burned out at least one complete square mile. Tokyo police records obtained by intelligence teams after the war showed that 28,000 buildings had been gutted or completely burned to ashes, and that casualties were "very bad."

There was one more attempt to launch a heavy precision attack. On March 4th Le May ordered the B-29's out for their eighth strike at the Musashino factory in Tokyo—a target that was defying all attempts at destruction. Not only had the B-29's smashed at Musashino seven times, but it had also been visited by a heavy carrier force.

The results didn't show the enormous effort expended—Musashino, in official evaluation, stood "virtually intact." The most powerful B-29 force directed against Musashino—192 of the heavyweights—went all out in the eighth B-29 attempt to destroy the vital plant.

Musashino came through the mission with little more than a scratch. Heavy clouds completely obscured the target area, and the Superfortresses dumped their bombs by radar—unable to observe any results.

The raid was a fiasco. The elaborately planned, extensive campaign to destroy the Japanese aircraft industry by daylight, high-altitude precision bombing—which had been regarded with the highest favor and hopes—had turned out to be a failure.

7

DECISION

The facts were there; they were disagreeable, distasteful, but undeniable. It was time for what the historians are so fond of calling an "agonizing reappraisal." For, no matter how the statistical cake was sliced, the precision-bombardment campaign still added up to failure.

There were eleven high-priority targets in Japan to be destroyed by the precision daylight attack with high-explosives bombs by the B-29's. By the end of the first week in March, 1945, not a single one of these targets had been destroyed. Akashi had been effectively crippled, it was true, and would never again contribute substantially to Japan's war effort; but even Akashi was not 100 per cent destroyed.

The Mitsubishi engine and assembly plants at Nagoya and at Nakajima-Ota had been hit hard enough to affect production seriously and cause a slowdown, but this, too, was a far cry from being "destroyed."

Nothing, however, embittered and frustrated the planners of the raids more than the continued production of the Musashino works. A total of 835 B-29's had been over the factory with scarcely any results. A single Naval carrier strike had done more damage than all the B-29 attacks to date, and the measure of the B-29's failure may be determined by the fact that despite all the raids Musashino had suffered only 4 per cent damage.

In 1944, with operations barely getting under way, there had not been a single mission on which 100 B-29's went out. In the first nine weeks of 1945, the average raid was up to only 130 planes per mission. Not only had the strategic precision-bombing campaign failed, but the first tests with incendiary bombs were largely inconclusive, and promised no better results in the destruction of Japanese industry.

Official reports marked "top secret" in Washington declared that "Japan's production capacity has not yet been fundamentally weakened." The use of the B-29 was coming in for more and sharper criticism. The situation had degenerated into a crisis.

There were, however, results that simply couldn't be measured on charts or graphs, and these constituted a very real diminishing of Japan's military industrial effort. Despite their category—"indirect results"—they affected the Japanese ability to sustain its fighting forces.

The fall of Saipan and the increasing weight of B-29 attacks influenced greatly the attitude of industrialists toward the war. The promise of a cascade of high explosives from the sky (even while the strategic planners of the XXI Bomber Command were expressing disgust at poor results of the campaign) so unnerved the Japanese that a hasty, ill-organized dispersal and underground program for the vital war plants was implemented. Conducted with far less efficiency than a similar effort in Germany, the dispersal program seriously affected Japanese production and cost Japan the equivalent of several totally devastating raids that would have destroyed entire factories. Dispersal so affected one fighter-plane factory, for example, that production fell from 300 to but 100 fighters each month—over a period of some four to six months.

But such considerations could not be brought into a hard and objective analysis of the B-29 campaign against Japan as carried out from the Marianas. In a total of 22 missions that placed an aggregate of 2,148 planes over Japan, the B-29's had dropped the disappointing total of only 5,398 tons of bombs. Barely half of all the Superfortresses that reached Japan struck their primary targets.

Losses were unexpectedly high, for in January we were losing 5.7 per cent of all bombers that became airborne. Because they attacked at an average height of

30,000 feet, the B-29's reduced greatly the effectiveness of Japanese anti-aircraft, which was designed to operate with deadly results at lower altitudes. In the early missions the fighters often proved ineffective; not all types of Japanese fighters could meet the B-29's on their own terms—great speed at high altitude. But because the bombers returned to certain specified targets, the Japanese tightened up their defenses, concentrated their fighters in these areas, and gave the B-29's "absolute hell."

A report from Saipan on this subject, dated 1945: "Fighter attacks grew more and more fierce, and they account for most of our losses over the target. At very high altitudes flak was generally too inaccurate to be effective. During the first high-altitude strikes (28,000 to 33,000 feet) on the Mitsubishi aircraft plant at north Nagoya, the B-29's were met by a total of 1,731 fighter attacks. Our gunners shot down 48, probably destroyed 50 others. And on the Wing's 14th strike against the Jap homeland on 27 January, 'fighter opposition of unparalleled intensity was met.' Fighter pilots in their combat reports tell how 'fanatical hopped-up pilots pressed their attacks right down the formations' stream of fire, dove into formations to attempt rammings, and sprayed fire at random.' Five B-29's went down over the target. Two ditched on the way home, and 33 returned with battle scars. . . . "

In the losses sustained from the first raid to the end of February, 1945, the Command lost twenty-nine B-29's to enemy fighters, one to flak, nine to a combination of fighters and flak, and another twenty-one bombers to operational difficulties. Fifteen went down to "unknown causes." Whatever the reason—the loss of seventy-five B-29 Superfortresses, with many of the crews, was a heavy blow.

Hindsight reveals that a fault existed in the concept of the strategic bombardment campaign against Japan. In Germany, the A.A.F. had fought a hard, grueling battle to conduct precision daylight bombing. Against the dire warnings of the British—who had suffered bloody losses in daylight raids and were forced to bomb at night—and facing the toughest fighter and flak opposition in the world, the B-17's and B-24's with fighter escort pounded German factories to rubble. The battle won in European skies was as

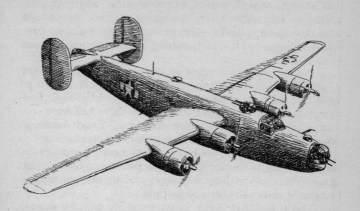

Liberator

much a victory of doctrine as it was of combat, and it was
natural that with the B-29, a superb bombing weapon, the
A.A.F. should continue this pattern against Japan.

The fault lay in the extreme differences of operating
conditions, *and especially in the nature of the targets.* Experts familiar with Japanese cities and the nature of the
country's industry were strongly recommending a con-
certed incendiary war from the air. But this meant rejecting
a system that had proven itself in battle, for a completely
new and untried (for the A.A.F.) method of attack.

This was no tactical exercise. The entire strategy of
the Pacific war hinged on the B-29 campaign against
Japan. It involved an investment of many billions of dollars, not only in the B-29 program, but in training, crews,
logistics, ad infinitum. Many men had died in order to win
the islands as B-29 bases, and many more died in the savage, bloody fight for Iwo Jima.

The crux of the matter lay in the specific construction
of the target cities. In Europe the cities and factories were
well built, of solid materials. The railroad system was outstanding. There were good roads. The Germans were mas-

ters at industrial dispersal, improvisation, and they possessed an incredible talent for springing back into action after devastating attacks. Against such targets the deep-penetration, high-explosive bombing campaign had proven successful.

But in Japan more than 90 per cent of the cities were of tinderbox construction. Concrete and steel buildings were rare outposts amid sprawling jungles of firetraps. Furthermore, in the hearts of these jungles there had been created a vast system of "shadow factories." Every Japanese home, it seemed, was a little factory for war production.

This point should not be underestimated; it exposes for the lie it truly is the contention that this was mass warfare against innocent civilians who were making no contribution to Japan's ability to continue its fight.

The Royal Air Force in its bombing attacks against Germany determined that the fifteen most critical targets contained some 12 per cent of the German labor force. But in Japan, at least 43 per cent of the labor force was concentrated within only fourteen leading urban areas.

The concentration of industry within these urban areas was almost beyond belief. Nagoya alone produced more than 40 per cent of all Japanese aircraft engines; more than half of all machine tools were made in four cities; 30 per cent of all aircraft assembly took place in two cities; 90 per cent of electronic manufacture was concentrated in three cities.

Destroy these cities and you destroyed Japan's ability to maintain industry. One third of all Japanese industry was in the "shadow factory" system—and another third of Japanese war production came from factories that employed thirty persons or less.

How to strike at the system? Precision bombing was useless—it would call first for identifying each individual home or building among an ocean of rooftops, and such accuracy was simply impossible. Precision bombing was essential, and would remain so until the very last day of war, but against those targets that demanded this specific means of attention—isolated and key factories and the solid, modern, fire-resistant combines within the cities.

There was no doubt that the first three months of the

B-29 campaign was a failure; even the leaders of the XXI Bomber Command recognized that fact. Six weeks after he took over the command of the organization, a disgruntled Le May in a disparaging remark to his public-relations officer, Lt. Colonel St. Clair McKelway, grumbled that: "This outfit has been getting a lot of publicity without having really accomplished a hell of a lot in bombing results."

Le May made this statement on March 6th. Four days later the sentence was no longer valid. Le May threw away the book, made the greatest gamble any air commander has ever made or is likely ever to have a chance of making, and brought utter catastrophe to Japan. The change was the decision to forfeit all that had gone before and to institute new tactics which, for the B-29, were both extraordinary and revolutionary.

The B-29 crews learned about the change on the morning of March 9th as they filed into the Quonsets and other buildings for the briefings on the raid. Like all briefings, it began in the usual manner. There came the sharp cry of *"Attention!"* Benches and chairs and shoes scraped the floor as hundreds of men rose to their feet. The group commanders and their staffs entered, clutching maps and notes, and walked to the raised platforms at the head of each room from where they would conduct the briefing.

The words are different in each of the huts, but the meaning is clear—and shocking. Perhaps one colonel starts by saying: "This time. . . . " Or he may begin with: "Our target tonight will be Tokyo. . . . " But from this point on there is close attention.

"We are throwing away the book," a colonel told his airmen, and instantly the room was just a little quieter than before, every man was sitting a bit straighter, listening carefully.

"This time we will not fly formations." A pause as the men turn to look at each other, or shrug their shoulders.

"We are going in at night. . . ."

In the B-29? At night, without formation? What the hell is *this*?

There is a pause that lasts longer than usual. The men lean forward.

"We will make our attacks at an altitude that extends from five thousand to seven thousand feet. . . ."

It is impossible for the men to remain quiet. There are startled exclamations, some curses. The men shift in their chairs, they wet their lips, suck nervously on cigarettes. The tension is now a living thing.

They learn that the bombs will be incendiaries, that Le May is sending the bombers in at minimum altitude with very heavy bomb loads to strew incendiaries across a ten-square-mile area in the heart of Tokyo. It will be an all-out, massive incendiary attack. It has never been done before.

"We will carry heavy bomb loads, about seven or eight tons per airplane. We can do this because you will go in to the target individually. There will be no assemblies, so you will not burn gas staging. Neither will you have to climb to high altitudes, and this also will reduce your fuel requirements. . . ."

Then comes the statement that freezes the room into absolute silence. "All guns except the tail cannon will be removed from your aircraft; in later missions this will also be removed."

No guns! It will be suicide!

What about flak when we come in on the deck; *they'll murder us!*

But it had all been planned very carefully. For the sake of history, let it be stated that General Curtis E. Le May was the one man who made the ultimate decision, who went against the strong recommendations of his closest aides, and who also was to be marked as one of the most able and daring bomber commanders of the entire war.

To obtain a firsthand report of the making of this decision, with the freshness of a contemporary account, here is the story as it came out of the Marianas in 1945, under the appropriate title of:

"TURNING POINT: GENERAL LE MAY'S GREAT DECISION"

. . . Against this background of poor conditions and poor results, it was decided to depart radically from the traditional doctrine of strategic bombardment. Just how radically was not known to most of the flyers until the memorable morning of 9 March when in all briefing rooms throughout the Marianas an announcement was made. It was followed by a sudden, shocked silence as the crews began to realize what they had just heard:

(1) A series of maximum effort night incendiary attacks were to be made on major Japanese industrial cities.

(2) Bombing altitudes would be from 5,000 to 8,000 feet.

(3) No armament or ammunition would be carried and the size of the crew would be reduced.

(4) Aircraft would attack individually.

(5) Tokyo, bristling with defenses, would be the first target.

"In making this daring decision, General Le May was not motivated simply by the desire to get better performance from his crews and aircraft. Nor were these operations conceived as terror raids against Japan's civilian population. The Japanese economy depended heavily on home industries carried on in cities close to major factory areas. By destroying these feeder industries, the flow of vital parts could be curtailed and production disorganized. A general conflagration in a city like Tokyo or Nagoya might have the further advantage of spreading to some of the priority targets located in those areas, making it unnecessary to knock them out by separate pinpoint attacks.

"Incendiary operations were not new. Several trials had been made. On some attacks a mixed load of H.E. and incendiary bombs had been used with indifferent results. On three missions prior to 9 March incendiaries alone were used. According to the Phase Analysis reports, these results, too, were indifferent. This was partly because the ballistic characteristics of incendiary clusters rendered them inaccurate when dropped from high altitudes in strong winds, partly because not enough B-29's had been available for a major strike against a big urban area. But by the start of March the 313th Wing had joined the 73rd Wing as a fully operational unit, and two groups from the 314th, recently arrived on Guam, were ready for action. Thus, the combined force now totaled more than 300 aircraft—enough to strike a spark.

"One main advantage in lowering the altitude to between 5,000 and 8,000 feet was the increased bomb load. A single B-29 flying in formation at high altitude could carry only 35 per cent of the possible bomb load of a B-29 attacking individually at the lower altitude. This was made possible, of course, because individual attacks required no assembly over the base at the mission's start or reassembly en route to the target. Aircraft would go directly from base to target and return, thus saving gas and allowing a greater bomb load. Better weather would be encountered at the lower altitude and the heavy, gas-consuming winds of high altitudes would be avoided. The weight of extra crew members, armament and ammunition would go into bombs. With the largest bomb load carried to date to Japan, each B-29 would bear six to eight tons, largely the new M-69 fire bomb, composed of an incendiary cluster containing a jelly-gasoline compound. It was felt that the weakness of Jap night fighters justified the elimination of armament.

"*Time* was a crucial element in the new plan.

"Jap night fighters were known to be weak, but flak losses were expected to be substantial. By making a night attack it was hoped to minimize these losses, since enemy radar gun-laying devices were though to be comparably inefficient, and heavy AA guns would thus have to depend on searchlights for effective fire control.

"It was found that the best time for takeoff was around dusk, so that the planes could benefit by at least some daylight for the getaway. This brought them to the target before dawn, and, most important, enabled them to make the homeward flight by daylight, thus avoiding night ditchings of battle-damaged aircraft.

"Finally, these missions had to be completed in time for the B-29's to coordinate their efforts with the naval strike at Okinawa. Since the first of the Okinawa operations was scheduled for 23 March, only a little more than two weeks were available in which to hit the four big targets—Tokyo, Nagoya, Osaka, Kobe.

"Viewed in retrospect, it appears that almost everything was in favor of the low-altitude night attacks. Nevertheless, it took extraordinary courage to risk 300 unarmed aircraft on a new type of attack directly opposed to the traditional doctrine of high-altitude precision bombing for which the B-29's had been expressly designed. The imagination, the flexibility of mind, the unwillingness to be bound by established precepts once they no longer proved applicable to the situation at hand—these qualities in our Air Force leadership contributed beyond measure to our victory, and were indeed our secret weapon.

"Probably no mission, except the first historic ones against Yawata and Tokyo, was sweated out with more anxiety than the 9 March strike on Tokyo. This time, in the event of failure, nobody could claim that we were pioneering against an unknown enemy. This time the risk of men and equipment was many times greater. This time it was later in the game and the need for decisive air action was more acute.

"On the afternoon of 10 March, when one by one the B-29's returned to the Marianas, the verdict became known. Pilots told how Tokyo 'caught fire like a forest of pine trees.'"

Thus Le May made his decision, and the die was cast for a flaming catastrophe that would descend upon the un-suspecting Japanese capital. In terms of history, in the usual procedure of committing so mighty a force to battle, the decision was not long and drawn out; although, indeed, it came very late in the scheduling of attacks.

On March 8th the field orders were out—only one day before the strike. Even though the XXI Bomber Command operated under Headquarters, Twentieth Air Force, in the Pentagon, General Arnold did not learn of the decision to strike with revolutionary tactics until some twenty-four hours prior to the mission.

According to Le May's orders the pathfinder B-29's, leading the way, were to be armed with 180 bombs—each an M47A2, 70-pound bomb filled with napalm and set to explode at 100 feet. The napalm showered outward at a hundred feet, stuck fast to whatever it hit, and started what are known as "appliance fires"—blazes calling for the at-tention of fire-fighting equipment.

The pathfinders were to strike four designated aiming

points, using radar to hit their exact targets. The B-29's that followed would each carry 24 500-pound bombs. These bombs scattered open in clusters at fifty feet, releasing a shower of the six-pound M-69 incendiaries.

To the crews, there was another, more ominous aspect of the briefings. Here are excerpts from that briefing of March 9th before the planes took off for Japan:

" . . . if you are crew members of a B-29, then you must expect to receive the roughest sort of treatment from the Japanese. What little information we have managed to accumulate indicates that if you are below the rank of lieutenant-colonel, then you will be required to perform labor as the Japanese direct and see fit. We don't have all the information we'd like so far, but what we've learned does show that if you are an officer the Japanese will likely treat you worse than they do the enlisted men. You will be interrogated more often and much more rigorously than you may have believed, because the Japanese feel that as officers you know more. If you fail to come across with the information they want—we're going to be blunt about this—then you'll stand a good chance of being given 'the business' until you break one way or the other.

"By international law you are required to give only your name, rank, and serial number, but the Japs aren't quite so careful about respecting international law one way or the other. They are desperately anxious to find out everything they can about the B-29, and it is likely that they will go to any lengths to do so. You are to tell them as little as possible, but don't—repeat—don't try to lie to them, or to be a smart guy and try to mislead them. They're too smart for that kind of business, and they're only going to make it very rough on you.

"If you are shot down, try and get picked up by the Japanese military just as quickly as possible. The civilians will kill you—right out. They will either club or stone you or shoot you. Some wounded crew members have been scalded to death with boiling water, others run through with knives. The military would like to do exactly the same, but usually they don't dare go that far because you are worth more to them alive than dead. At least, that is until they can get all the information out of you they think is possible.

Then, it's not at all unlikely that they will kill you anyway. They've done it before too many times for us to entertain any hopes that guarantee you any rights as a prisoner.

"If you're shot up over the mainland and you've got to come down, always—repeat—always go for the water. Try to avoid a crash landing on the islands if at all possible. The Japanese army and the navy don't like each other, they're mad at each other, and their navy will treat you much better than the army. The navy blames these bombings you're giving Japan on the army, and is doing its best to discredit the local opposition. There's even a chance that they'll refuse to turn you over to the army for some time. In the meantime you'll be a lot better off—better fed and housed.

"Now, if you are taken prisoner—*never*—repeat—*never* call a Jap, a Jap. It is always a Japanese, and say it with respect. Give him some lip or call him a Jap and he'll take your head right off.

"The Japanese have killed prisoners, and they won't hesitate to kill more of them. Many of the people who were killed were the ramrod, stiff-necked West Point types who fell into their hands earlier in the war. They got nasty and the Japanese very calmly either shot them or cut off their heads.

"Don't ever get nasty with a Jap. Don't ever forget that rule. They thrive on politeness in their personal relationships and you've simply got to be even more polite. Odds are you'll be interrogated by a sergeant. Treat him as if he were God. And he is, under those conditions, your infinite superior. Act like it and you improve your chances of living——"

"Which isn't very goddamned good to begin with if you're a prisoner," interrupted a gunner in the briefing audience.

"Amen," said a few hundred airmen.

8

TOKYO

The great area in the midst of the Japanese capital that was to receive its trial by fire was known to the citizens of Tokyo as Shitamachi—or downtown.

The old city limit of Tokyo was divided roughly by the Sumida River, which flows from north to south, into Tokyo Bay. On the western side of the river the land rises to an elevation above sea level of perhaps two hundred feet. This section is named Yamate, which, roughly translated, means bluff or uptown. The eastern side of the Sumida with its congested, narrow streets, lies in the low section of Tokyo and is known as the downtown area.

"The northern part of the eastern side," explains Fred Saito, "was called the Honjo Ward, and the southern half the Fukagawa Ward. Both sectors teemed with the shops of small merchants, and the small home machine shops—or 'shadow factories,' as you call them.

"Asakusa, an amusement center, is another downtown area that is directly across the river from the Honjo Ward. East of Fukagawa is the Nihonbashi, a major area for wholesalers in supplies, foods, and similar goods. All four of these wards were completely devastated in the attack.

"Tokyo's biggest business and political administration center stood further west of Nihonbashi. In the uptown section of the capital were the main residential sections for the white-collar workers and the wealthy of Tokyo. On the first major raid some scattered incendiary bombs hit this section, but it escaped with little damage. The people considered themselves fortunate, but later the fires of subsequent attacks wiped out these sections as well.

"To many of the seven hundred thousand people who lived and worked in the downtown section of Tokyo, the first heavy incendiary raid seemed like a repetition of the terrible fires that followed the great earthquake of September 1st in 1923. These people learned a great deal about a mass fire after that earthquake, of course; unhappily for them, however, the lessons proved completely worthless in the face of the overwhelming fire-bombing from the sky.

"The bombing of March 10th wasn't the first incendiary raid that Tokyo had known. But the previous attacks gave no warning of the calamity that was about to hit the city. When the B-25's of Doolittle's attack flew over Tokyo in April of 1942, the event was so unexpected that all Japan talked about it for months. But everyone realized that it was basically a morale strike—more to bolster the morale of the American people than to hurt our own—and by 1945 they had just about forgotten the event.

"The attacks of 1944—the last two months of that year—weren't damaging enough to alarm us. On February 25th of 1945, about a hundred and thirty B-29's raided the city from great altitude. Most of the bombs fell in the factory areas or in the surrounding countryside. The damage was slight, the casualties low. It was snowing that day, and the people were more interested in the bombing than frightened by what could happen.

"There were other raids before this one, during the month of February. But the one strike that really unnerved the people was the carrier assault of February 16th. It seemed that a thousand or more planes were racing around central Honshu, mostly around Tokyo and Yokohama, flying right over the housetops. The sky was black with planes—everywhere you looked you could see them. But again the damage wasn't great.

"It's too bad that it wasn't worse. Casualties after all these attacks had remained so low that not only the government officials, but the man in the street, came to consider these as the 'American pattern of attacks against which we can certainly stand up.' The defense plans lapsed into a complacency that later acted as a killer of those same people, so sudden and so overwhelming was the massive night incendiary strike."

In early 1945, downtown Tokyo was dismal and drab. This area particularly was an eyesore; it had never had the community spirit to improve its appearance to outsiders, and in truth had all the unwholesomeness of a great slum area neglected by its citizens. Under wartime conditions it was depressing to the eye.

On the main streets there existed a funereal atmosphere; most of the streets were empty of traffic. Three quarters of a million people still lived and worked in downtown Tokyo but the majority of the stores were closed down, the doors locked and the windows boarded. Certainly many of the stores had little purpose in remaining open; precious little was left to sell. The terrible effectiveness of the American submarines in the Pacific, augmented by a relentless aerial attack against shipping and an intensive aerial mining campaign, had closed Japan off from its conquests except for a trickle of urgent raw materials.

Food was scarce, and the people were obviously undernourished. Wan and drawn, they were tired of ceaseless claims of conquest that were obviously untruthful. The war with China had been going on for eight years. The Americans had been fighting already for four years, and it was no longer possible to believe in Japan's invincibility. The B-29's were overhead and the carrier planes, when they came, flew over in swarms, disdainful of all Japanese defenses. There were still exhortations—from loudspeakers that blared at corners, on home radios, in newspapers, and on giant posters—for a final all-out effort to destroy the Americans. And surprisingly, the Japanese people did believe that "eventually" Japan would marshal some inner strength and emerge the victor from its war. In the interim, however, they grew increasingly weary with shortages and privation, and the increase in the size of the B-29 formations did their emotional make-up no good.

Japanese cities are famous for their thousands of trees; no matter where the visitor travels he will always find trees. But not in downtown Tokyo. The flimsy, inflammable wooden and bamboo houses were largely in disrepair. Garbage collection had deteriorated as well, and hygienic standards had fallen far below the usual high norm for the Japanese.

But in virtually every back alley there was a constant, humming activity that went on twenty-four hours a day. Here were the shadow factories, the lathes, punch-presses, the drills—all the ingredients of a sprawling, unseen industrial force working around the clock. In this respect the people of Tokyo, even in its worst sections, never knew rest. Twelve-hour shifts were replaced immediately with a second working force. Downtown Tokyo was drab, listless, emotionally sallow—but it worked day and night.

In this section of the capital several large streets, some fifty yards across, cut a swath through the teeming jungle of congestion. The average wooden building was a square of twenty yards by twenty yards. They stood one against the other in an incredible profusion that must be seen to be believed.

Most of the school children had been evacuated to the outlying provinces under government order. But in downtown Tokyo the people simply could not afford to send their children, wives, and old people out of the city. Thus the majority of the inhabitants—mothers with small children, the aged and infirm—were horribly susceptible to most fire attack.

The Japanese government did not accept responsibility for the masses of people who had not been evacuated. These people broke government edict, but the officials were not quick to enforce their rules, especially in the slum areas.

One government order was enforced, however. Every house and building in downtown Tokyo had its own private dugout, something on the order of a soldier's foxhole. Each of these dugouts was barely large enough to accommodate a family on the sounding of an air-raid alarm, and their value was negligible. But the government ordered them to be built, enforced its orders with police—and they were built. As events proved, it was all wasted effort.

Also as a result of government edict, each house and

building contained an oil drum or a bathtub, or some similar container, filled with water. City and government officials honestly believed that these measures would suffice to restrict fire development. It was a case of thinking in terms of minor blazes instead of catastrophic flames the size and fury of which Tokyo had never known.

Beginning late in 1944 and continuing until just before the end of the war in August of 1945, the Japanese pressed a system of firebreaks in the center of their largest cities. These were made by the simple expedient of tearing down wooden structures in certain areas so as to form lanes 36 to 120 feet wide through sections where the flames would be most likely to spread because of building congestion. In five cities, the Japanese demolished 346,629 buildings.

In downtown Tokyo an elevated train ran from east to west. Along this line the buildings were ripped down, using the elevated as the center of the firebreak. This wide avenue was still incomplete when the heavy incendiary raid came; those who ran to the completed end and could reach areas free of the flames survived—the others were jammed together, and were much less fortunate.

Most of the fire lanes planned for downtown Tokyo had not been finished by March 9th; the people in the area were told by their officials that "because of a lack of funds, many of the plans now on paper will be brought to reality some time in 1946."

It was a fatal error of the city officials of Tokyo to put their faith entirely in their inadequate firebreak protection. Most of these protective lanes—in downtown Tokyo as well as elsewhere in the city—had serious basic weaknesses. When the Japanese ordered homeowners to tear down their buildings, the owners were only partially reimbursed for their losses, and were understandably loath to tear down what had been patiently built up over a period of years. In some cases, if the house or store was costly—or more important, if the owner had political influence—this single dwelling would be left to protrude into the firebreak itself, a fiery wall to block the flight of refugees.

There was yet another weakness in the firebreak system. Many of the stores and dwellings along street fronts had imitation stone, metal-clad, or stucco facing as a protection against exposure fires; removing these structures to make firebreaks actually exposed other buildings behind them that had unprotected fronts.

PATTERN OF THE CITY AND ITS BUILDINGS

Despite a long history of major fires in their principal cities, the Japanese showed a marked lack of progress in fire fighting. The earthquake and subsequent fire in Tokyo in 1923 is well known, but there were other mass conflagrations as well. Large parts of Tokyo were destroyed in 1925 and 1932. Enormous fires blazed up in Niigata (1925), Yamanaka (1931), Hakodate (1934), and Takaoka (1938), to name but a few.

Certainly the explosive combustibility of Japanese buildings has been the major contributing factor to these disasters. The typical Japanese dwelling was a flimsy one- or two-story frame building with a tile roof. Floors were one-half inch boards covered by tatamis—rice-straw mats. Walls were made of bamboo laths thickly coated on both sides with a natural cement mud, and exterior sides were covered by wide unpainted lapboard.

When conditions permitted there was at least three feet of space between buildings. In downtown Tokyo, however, the structures were jammed together in a jumbled profusion. Eaves had so much overhang that they pressed against nearby buildings. In the slum section most buildings stood wall to wall without any space between them. There were no true streets, only narrow, twisting alleys through which rapid flight was impossible.

The commercial structures were largely of two-story frame construction. Even the substantial fire-resistant department stores were crammed with highly combustible merchandise.

As the nation's capital, Tokyo had some load-bearing brick-wall commercial buildings similar to buildings in the United States. However, they were generally naked to assault by fire because they lacked such exposure protection devices as wire-glass windows, shutters, outside water curtains, and fire doors. Noncombustible structures of corrugated iron or asbestos cement on light steel frames were generally similar to those of Western construction. These were found, however, only in industrial plants, and they were invariably deathtraps because of their highly combustible and explosive contents.

Some lessons were taken to heart from the history of mass, destructive fires, and Tokyo (as well as all other leading cities) was dotted with the modern earthquake-resistant building that was one of the most massive buildings in the world, made of extra-heavy reinforced concrete. Roofs and floors had minimum thickness of six inches, and some had nine- to fourteen-inch concrete roofs. Heavy haunches and outside buttresses made them appear additionally strong and invulnerable.

Yet, here again, the inexplicable thinking of the Japanese asserted itself. Fire-resistive construction stopped with the basic structure of the building, for the interiors—wood-lath and plaster partitions, suspended ceilings, wood-overlay floors with air spaces beneath, wood-trim stairways, handrails, and even doorknobs—were especially susceptible to fire. And there was seldom provided any adequate protection for outside wall openings.

During the fire bombings of Japan, the ability of these structures to remain standing despite the intense fires discouraged the intelligence officers of the XXI Bomber Command, who believed that the buildings were still intact. It was not until the war was over and our teams moved into Tokyo and other cities that we learned that while the roofs and walls remained standing in a sea of devastation, the interiors of more than three out of every four such buildings were completely gutted.

FIRE DEFENSES

Regardless of their size, Japan's cities were densely built up, and Tokyo with its teeming population of more than seven million people (1939 census) was actually the worst of all the country's urban areas. There were in the city some 22.5 square miles of residential area with a building density of 46 per cent—in a given area, 46 per cent of the total ground area was occupied by buildings. The industrial sections of Tokyo averaged more than 40 per cent

building density, and the mixed residential and manufac-
turing areas—the downtown section—as high as 50 per cent.

The Japanese had yet to learn—since before the night
of March 10th they had not faced B-29's carrying up to
eight tons of bombs—that the incendiary-bomb load of one
Superfortress could create many individual fires simultaneously. These merged with almost unbelievable speed, and
with a matter of minutes an area of 600 feet by 2,000 feet
was a mass of roaring flame. The lethal aspect of such a
salvo was that within a very few minutes after the incendiaries sprayed away from their canisters, *people in the center of the area would be completely cut off from escape.*

To their grave sorrow the Japanese had seriously mis-
judged our ability to attack in heavy force with the B-29's.
Recognizing the danger of incendiary attack, the government had laid down some building rules that would eventually have improved the fire resistance of the cities, but
these were not pressed with any enthusiasm and most of
the regulations were simply ignored.

There existed a vast difference, therefore, in the defensive measures of the Japanese and German cities. A
comparison of Hamburg (see *The Night Hamburg Died*)
and Tokyo reveals that the German port city was probably
the best defended urban area in the world. A strict and intelligent police-fire organization controlled the efforts of a
people eager to comply with the rules established for their
own protection. Had not Hamburg been swept by an incredible firestorm, the damage from even so severe an attack as the British carried out in Operation Gomorrah
would likely have been much less.

Tokyo, unhappily, suffered seriously by its deficiency
in fire protection, and the reasons for this gross failure are
unusual and most interesting. Despite the combustibility of
the individual Japanese homes and buildings—and thus the
entire city area—there were normally many fewer fires in
Tokyo than in a comparable city in the United States. Para-
doxical as it seems, it is understandable with knowledge of
the Japanese.

Unlike our system, fire in Japan was a punishable

criminal offense, and the party responsible for allowing a fire to begin was held liable for all the fire damage done to his neighbors' homes. Thus fire-prevention entailed harsh economic pressures. There is nothing quite so likely to endow the citizenry with caution as the application of stern measures to the pocketbook, and this was precisely the situation in Japan.

But at the same time, this success with preventing the small, local fire created complacency about the development of major fire-fighting systems or organizations. In Tokyo, there was a severe shortage of fire-fighting equipment. Indeed, the trucks and other equipment were, on the average, so inefficient that any small-town volunteer fire department in the United States would have rejected them as useless. Almost all the effective fire-fighting equipment in Japan had been purchased originally from either the United States of Germany, and this supply had been completely cut off for years. The result was a fire-fighting system that was ill-equipped, badly trained, and generally incapable of doing much more than putting on a good deal of pomp and then fleeing for their own lives. Again it is a peculiarity of the Japanese that must be stressed—the men were extraordinarily brave (I have seen Japanese firemen in action many times and will personally attest to their remarkable courage and heroism), but their efforts were outlandishly inefficient.

The Tokyo fire department in 1945 was an organization that would have driven its contemporaries in this country to complete distraction. The police in Japan have always been all-powerful, and the firemen resented bitterly the high-handed manner in which the police both controlled their organization and pushed them around. The Japanese social caste system is something that must be seen to be believed, and the question of "saving face" preempted all other considerations.

Leadership among the fire-fighting units was appalling. The need for soldiers stripped the cities of able-bodied men, and only those too young to wear a uniform or physically unfit to serve were at home to defend the cities.

In times of peace the Tokyo fire department normally numbered about 2,000 men; by March of 1945 this figure had been increased to more than 8,000. An attempt was made to bring 5,000 more men into the organization, but the manpower shortage was prohibitive.

The total of 8,000—including 2,700 "junior firemen" between the ages of 13 and 17 years—had to care for a metropolitan district of 213 square miles and more than seven and a half million people! And they had to do this with crowded streets, explosively combustible buildings, ancient fire equipment, an almost leaderless organization— all in all it was a sorry mess.

Prewar training for new recruits with the full-time fire department of Tokyo included three months of school and practice; in early 1945, this was pared to but thirty days. But it would have mattered little had their training extended for a year, for strangely enough the courses in actual fire-fighting were the least of the curriculum! Emphasized primarily were military drills with goose-stepping and saluting; pomp and circumstance were far more important than an ability to fight fire.

Equipment was so short that the schools used dummy materials for their drills. The recruit firemen in Tokyo, as an example, took their positions on a decommissioned fire pump as if they were rolling to a fire. At a given command, they very precisely removed a hose-reel cart from the hose bed, reeled out 131 feet of hose (two sections), connected the hose section to the pumper, then laid two sections of hose back to the apparatus. It took seven men to perform this operation, and if that number of men were not present, the whole drill was simply abandoned as impossible!

And to cap the absurdity of it all, the firemen never deviated from this standard during the height of the bombing attacks.

Much of the time devoted to training recruits was spent in endless lectures on how vital it was for a fireman to be brave. It mattered little if the fireman knew virtually nothing about how to combat flames, just so long as he charged right into the roaring conflagration and put on a good show. Unlike their contemporaries in England and in Germany, who often braved the worst of air attack to fight flames, the Japanese firemen—admitted their chiefs—

showed no hesitation in running pell-mell for cover when high-explosive bombs came down with the incendiaries.

And there was that quirk in Japanese thinking all over again. They were brave in fighting fires, but nothing was ever said to them about being brave *while they were being bombed*. Once the B-29's were gone, they would all leap to the cause—but while so much as a single high-explosive bomb was going off, it was every man for himself and to hell with the fires.

At the peak of its defense, Tokyo had 12 fire divisions, 44 battalion districts, and 287 fire stations. It also had, in 1945, a total of 1,117 pieces of fire apparatus (compared to 280 pieces in 1943). In all of Japan there were only four aerial ladders, and three of these were in Tokyo. However, only one of the Tokyo ladder trucks—a German Magirus with an 85-foot extension—was in service. The two Japanese-built 100-foot aerials had motors that wouldn't work and turntables that jammed continually.

The Tokyo fire department used 2.5-inch hose of unlined linen, the majority of which was so old and worn out and full of patches that at pressures exceeding 100 pounds it was likely to burst.

Such equipment as trucks, appliances, pumpers, generators, lights, and special tools—so common to the small American fire department—was almost totally lacking in the biggest city in Japan. *Never* a part of the Tokyo fire department were special mobile rigs and companies, such as salvage, lights, CO_2, foam, rescue, demolition, airfield crash rigs, or even water tanks with booster pumps. Even the common portable fire extinguishers of the CO_2 type, or carbon-tetrachloride, foam, and water pump can models were never seen by the Japanese firemen.

Twenty per cent or more of existing apparatus was always out of service. Much of the equipment was defective, spare parts were in short supply, and the shortage of skilled mechanics was critical. In Tokyo, all fire trucks had to be hand cranked in starting. And when the fire stations answered a call, it was hell-bent-for-leather, without a single piece of apparatus standing by in reserve.

Until the searing raid of March 10th, each fire company was also restricted to a two-hour gasoline supply. In

Osaka, on March 14th, this particular plan of operations caused the loss of 48 pieces of fire equipment—they had no fuel to be driven out of the way of advancing flames, and so were consumed.

Typifying the terrible state of disrepair and general disorganization is the instance when different prefectures (similar to our counties) would come to the aid of one another in times of disaster. On one occasion, one prefecture sent sixty pumpers to a burning city 22 miles away. So many trucks broke down or just ran out of gasoline that only *two* pumpers arrived!

The Keibodan organization, an auxiliary police and fire unit set up to assist the regular fire and police departments, was another example of poor training in fire-fighting and of equipment little better than worthless. They were fumbling, erratic, irresponsible, and, of course, very brave—and foolish.

Water supplies were generally weak and depended largely on electrically operated, direct pumping systems with little or no reservoir capacities. Water mains and fire

Shiden

hydrants were too few and too small for extensive use in fire-fighting. Tokyo had a storage capacity of only eight gallons per person, while Akashi had two gallons per person. Nagoya was the only city that had anything resembling an adequate water supply, but even here the city was notoriously weak compared with the average of 250 gallons per person per day common in American cities in the 1940's.

Perhaps the best illustration of the capabilities of the fire department occurred in the city of Hachioji. Bombers had dropped thousands of leaflets warning of an impending raid, and as a result the city of Tokyo sent fifty of its largest type pumper trucks and 300 professional firemen to assist the local department. The next day, the greatest known concentration of men and equipment (55 trucks per square mile) ever gathered to fight a fire in any of the Japanese urban attacks was ready and waiting. Plans were made for the deployment of equipment and communications between companies, and the stage was set to wage a well-organized, epochal fight.

The water supply for the underground mains consisted of a filled 2,750,000 gallon reservoir on a hill. Three electrically driven pumps, each of 2,000 gallon capacity, were arranged to pump water from the river to the reservoir or directly into the mains.

Within fifteen minutes after the attack began, a cluster of bombs hit the electric switch station and knocked out all electric power. The public water pumps failed so that the only supply for the underground system was the reservoir, which was exhausted in ninety minutes. Fifteen trucks were driven onto the sand beach of the river, but the river was so low that no more trucks could get to the shallow beach pools, and relaying of the water wasn't even attempted. A number of the trucks caught fire, hose was burned, and one truck had its motor knocked out by a direct hit with an incendiary bomb.

The fire raged almost without opposition. It spread across all the main streets and before it burned out it had gutted two-thirds of the entire city.

But most symptomatic of the ritualistic nature of Japanese fire-fighting was the emphasis placed on the man known as the standard bearer. It was this individual's responsibility (for which he was feted as a hero) to carry the standard of the fire company to a point where the firemen had determined they were going to stop the spread of a fire.

The man entrusted with the standard represents the unflagging spirit of conquest of flames that sustains the company firemen. For his is the startling task at times to jump into the fire—and to stand there, hair smoking and clothes singed—thus demonstrating to the other men that *this* is the line at which the fire must be stopped.

The standard bearer could not leave his post until the fire was definitely extinguished. No matter if his clothes finally did burn and he began to roast alive. If he succumbed to the pain of the flames and ran, he became an outcast upon whom people spat. So great was the fear of public contempt that some standard bearers actually chose to perish in the flames.

Those who survived truly became giants among men, and could walk the streets with great pride.

It was all very courageous, and it helps to explain to some extent why in a period of six hours more people lost their lives by fire in Tokyo than at any other time in the history of mankind.

9

FIGHTERS AND FLAK

"I could have been wrong," said Major General Curtis E. Le May, speaking of the massive force of 334 B-29's assembled on Saipan, Tinian, and Guam to strike Tokyo in darkness. "But I reasoned, from a study of photographic intelligence, that Japan was poorly prepared for low-altitude night attack. She had little in the way of radar equipment or anti-aircraft guns. I wanted to take advantage of her weakness, and to exploit it for all it was worth. If the course had been over Germany, I know we couldn't have got by with it. German anti-aircraft was too deadly. For complete success in Japan, bomb tonnage had to be sufficient to saturate the area. With three wings in operation, we now had the necessary striking force."

History stood by General Le May, as we shall soon see.

"The Doolittle air raid of April, 1942," explains Major General Masatake Okumiya, "spurred plans to strengthen Japan's homeland defense against future bombings. Ever since the start of the war homeland defense had been the Army's responsibility, with the Navy relegated strictly to cooperate with the Army at the latter's convenience. The April 18th attack brought forth a government order that henceforth both services would take every measure to create an effective air defense. . . ."

The defensive measures for the next two years, however, were essentially of a passive nature, concentrating upon home-defense activities; little actually was done to increase the number of fighter planes that would stand by to intercept raids against the homeland. There were two reasons for this lack, the first being that the Japanese really did not believe a repetition would take place for a long time, if at all. Second, the Japanese had been battered mercilessly in the air along most of their fighting fronts. Midway cost them several hundred fighters, the air battles at Guadalcanal increased the graveyard of downed Japanese aircraft, and the Solomons and Rabaul areas proved a catastrophe of attrition that steadily whittled down available fighter strength.

The Japanese simply had failed to anticipate their devastating losses in fighters (to say nothing of their bombers), and the armed forces needed every available machine on the active combat line. As the war progressed, the Japanese, even under their total censorship, could not fail to recognize that the battle was approaching the homeland; the cry for air defense became stronger, especially from the industrialists. Despite this rising clamor little could be done; every airplane was needed to stem what had become a terrible steamroller of American air strength.

By the summer of 1943 Japanese planners were in a slight state of panic, having received their first accurate intelligence reports of the B-29 bomber. The first B-29 attack against Yawata on June 15th, 1944, has been covered in detail previously in this book. The Japanese reaction as it involved their homeland defense, however, is pertinent to this moment: "Despite its lack of destructive results," stated General Okumiya, "the first Yawata attack had a grave psychological effect on the Japanese people. Where they regarded the Doolittle raid as a nuisance, the Yawata assault promised tremendous bombing raids in the future. All Japan discussed what might happen when the Americans increased the severity of their raids. The iron chain the enemy was closing on the homeland was becoming ever tighter."

The Japanese intelligence system in China was remarkably capable, and well before the first B-29's appeared over Yawata the military knew that the first raids were about to start.

"Every bombing followed a certain pattern," continues Okumiya, "from which we could determine in advance of the attack how many planes would make the raids, when the attack would come, and other details of the missions. Because of this advance information, our mainland defense forces were able to have their fighters in the air waiting for the bombers as they arrived for their bomb runs.

"Our first information came two to three days before the attacks. American transport planes increased their shuttle flights between a British air base near Calcutta, India, and the B-29 fields in China, ferrying gasoline and other materials for the big planes. Our radio listening stations in Tokyo caught the details of every coded communication which, we determined, were from the American planes reporting the exact times of their arrivals and departures. These radio communications were so clear that we would calculate the exact number of planes flying the China missions."

Hayate

The Japanese system was incredible, for within two or three days the predicted number of B-29's would appear over Japan. Not once did this intelligence system fail, and whatever deductions were received from the system were flashed to units scattered throughout China for verification. Ten minutes after the last word was received, every fighter base and anti-aircraft unit knew the estimated arrival time of the B-29's.

With such a system in the hands of German pilots, the B-29's might have suffered terrifying losses. But this was not a low-flying bomber, or an airplane that dawdled along in the sky. The Japanese were almost unbelievably fortunate in anticipating the B-29's, but here their luck ran out. The first three attacks came at night, and both the Japanese army and navy were sorely deficient in night-fighter equipment, crews, techniques—in short, they had no effective defense. Those navy fighters that were scrambled were hard pressed to reach the B-29 bombing altitude, and their performance at six miles or higher was so poor that they could barely stay in the sky with the bombers, let alone perform effective attacks.

It was not until August 20th that the Japanese were able to make their first effective interception. More than forty fighters were airborne, most with auxiliary tanks to permit climb to altitude and enough fuel remaining for combat. Rather than pursue the B-29's, the fighters were able to dive from a slight advantage of height into the American formations. One B-29 fell to the massed attack, several others were damaged.

The airplane that proved successful was the navy's heavy, powerful, twin-engined *Gekko,* one of the very few fighters in Japan able to climb to great heights and to retain its performance at 30,000 feet and above. In addition, the airplanes were heavily armed with 20-mm. cannon. To assure effective operation of the fighter, the navy brought back to Japan its most experienced night-fighter pilots who had proven their ability in attacks against B-17's and B-24's in the Pacific.

In the spring of 1944, when they first recognized the threat of the B-29 bomber offensive, the Japanese completely reorganized their General Defense Headquarters in Tokyo. The army maintained three air brigades of fighters attached to their ground districts; in an administrative move to enhance the role of these organizations the brigades were raised to divisional status. An attempt was made to integrate both army and navy fighter forces into a single, closely coordinated interceptor defense; it failed in the face of long-standing enmity between the two services. The army set up its First Air Army, which was strictly a last-ditch, emergency unit that would, upon call, strip fighter planes from the training fields of Japan.

In August about 400 fighters were available for homeland defense. Of this total the navy had 192 machines, mostly Zero day fighters; a small number of *Raiden* and *Shiden* high-performance, cannon-armed fighters; and the *Gekko* night-fighter units. Forty-eight day and 24 night fighters were assigned to Yokosuka; 48 day and 12 night fighters to Kure; 48 day and 12 night fighters to Sasebo.

The army's forces included 110 fighters of all types and ages based in the Tokyo area; 60 fighters in northern Kyushu; 30 fighters in Osaka. In addition to all these planes, there were several hundred army and navy fighters assigned as escorts for bombers to attack American ships near the homeland. If there was time during an alert, many of these fighters could be thrown into the defense.

The total number of fighters in the islands, however, is not an accurate reflection of what constituted the *effective operational interceptor force*. Considering all factors—maintenance, serviceability, pilots, and so forth—the effective fighter force came to only some 400 airplanes.

During this period of fluctuation and buildup of strength, the XXI Bomber Command intelligence officers were finding it impossible to assess accurately the air defenses that would confront the Superfortresses. On October 12th, 1944, for example, the Pentagon estimated to the XXI Bomber Command staff that the Japanese had available as a front-line fighter force a total of 1,114 machines. Three weeks later Washington revised its figures down to 608 fighters; both estimates were too high.

On November 21, according to Japanese records, the

first deliberate ramming took place. Over Sasebo, Lieutenant Mikihiko Sakamoto dove his fighter into a B-29.

After the heavy precision attacks against the Japanese aircraft factories, the navy took emergency measures to gain in air strength. One hundred fighters went to Atsugi air base; these included *Zeros, Raidens, Shidens, Gekkos,* and *Gingas* (remodeled night fighters). Southeast of Nagoya, at the Meiji air base, the navy had only fifteen Zero fighters. To defend the Osaka and Kobe areas, there were but thirty Zeros, these operating from the Naruo air base.

The army had also increased its defensive fighter force; for both day and night operations it had two hundred planes in the Tokyo area. These included *Hayabusas, Shokis, Hiens, Hayates, Toryus,* and some bombers remodeled to carry fixed 20-mm. cannon. Nagoya had eighty fighters, and Osaka and Kobe some fifty airplanes.

Ramming had increased among the pilots, who found that their airplanes were—in official Japanese reports— "generally ineffective against the fast, high-flying, and powerfully armed B-29's." On December 3rd, 1944, three B-29's were rammed by army fighters, but a new twist was added. Two of the Japanese pilots managed to bail out just before their airplanes struck the American bombers, thus accomplishing their mission but living to fly and fight another day.

One of the best insights to the Japanese air defense operation is provided in the narrative of the squadron leader of the 302nd Navy Air Corps, based at Atsugi, which helped to defend the Tokyo area. The squadron leader, Lieutenant Teramura, describes a mission on February 2nd, 1945:

"At 28,000 feet I found a nine-plane formation of B-29's. I flew parallel to the bombers in an attempt to get in front of them and, finally, pulled ahead of the enemy planes, which kept up a constant fire at my fighter. I could see only a few tracers which drifted slowly toward me in parabola, and I felt little danger.

"About three thousand feet ahead of the B-29's I turned sharply and picked up speed in a shallow dive, dropping below the bombers and then pulling up for the attack. I opened fire against the first B-29 in the formation, attacking from the lower front side of the airplane. As the two planes closed rapidly I did not have the opportunity to maintain a long burst. The nose turrets of three B-29's surrounded my fighter with tracers. I opened fire and watched the tracer shells of my four cannon converge on the bomber ahead of me. When I was extremely close to the giant bomber I kicked right rudder and pushed the control stick forward and to the right, dropping away from the B-29 in a diving turn. My shells had struck home, for one of the B-29's engines was burning fiercely.

"One of my pilots, Harukawa, followed my plane and executed the same attack. Taking advantage of our diving speed, we turned and climbed to attack the bombers from below and behind. One of the B-29's dropped out of the formation, trailing a thick plume of white smoke from the outer left engine. Jettisoning its bombs, the airplane took a southeast course, toward the Pacific Ocean, steadily losing altitude in an attempt to escape our attack. I continued firing but soon exhausted my cannon-shell supply. Our *Raiden* fighters, however, were equipped with a single 20-mm. cannon mounted to the left and behind the pilot's seat, fixed to fire upward at an angle of thirty degrees. Diving to the attack from the right and behind the bomber, I closed the distance between our planes. By this time Harukawa had expended his ammunition and was returning to base.

"The enemy gunners kept up a steady defensive fire. I continued to pursue the bomber until I reached the ocean; by then my fuel was almost gone. When finally I turned to head for home, the B-29 was still trailing heavy smoke and descending almost to sea level. I doubted whether it could return to its base.

"I made an emergency landing at the Kohnoike Naval Air Base, where the mechanics discovered that enemy bullets had damaged my plane's engine and oil cooler."

Discussions with Japanese fighter pilots and intelligence officers who commanded homeland fighter defenses reveal that the more knowledgeable of the Japanese never truly believed that they had the means to stop the fleets of B-29's. Even before the mass night attacks, it had become

Raiden

all too obvious that the Japanese needed desperately a close-knit organization of air defense, and this was sorely lacking; moreover, the intrinsic differences between the army and navy seemed to preclude any true efficiency in such an organization.

By the beginning of 1944, the Japanese navy fighter force was still dependant on the Zero; improved over the original models, but lacking the performance to constitute a major threat to the B-29. The Mitsubishi *Raiden* was the first fighter designed essentially as a defender of the home islands; its characteristics were all suited for fighting heavy bombers like the B-29. It was fast, and for its purpose an excellent aircraft; many Japanese pilots considered the *Raiden* comparable to the Focke-Wulf FW-190 in effectiveness as an interceptor. Four 20-mm. cannon, a speed of more than 400 miles per hour, and steel armor plate made it a formidable opponent.

Unfortunately the *Raiden* suffered in other respects. Japanese pilot quality had fallen off greatly since the early days of the war, and there were too few veterans who could handle the *Raiden* with high skill—which the fighter demanded. Accustomed to aerobatic agility, the Japanese pilots complained that "compared to the Zero, it flew like a truck." Losses in training were appalling—and later in the war, when Mustangs and Hellcats swept over the islands, the inability of the *Raiden* to maneuver caused severe pilot casualties.

To bolster its strength and to provide at least one major unit of outstanding skill, the navy formed a new Matsuyama Wing. The best fighter pilots of the navy were assembled in Japan, and assigned the new *Shiden* fighters. With a speed greater than 420 miles per hour, highly maneuverable, armed with four 20-mm. cannon and protected by armor plate, the *Shiden* was a deadly weapon in the hands of the fighter-pilot aces of the Matsuyama Wing.

It was during these last months of the war that most of the remaining great pilots of Japan went to their deaths. Shoichi Sugita, the greatest living pilot in Japan, was killed when U.S. Navy fighters exploded his *Shiden* while Sugita was attempting to take off from Kanoya in southern Kyushu in the midst of a raid.

Kinsuke Muto, who became famous in Japan with his four officially credited kills of B-29 bombers, transferred to Okinawa after fighting over the homeland. He was shot down by a P-51 escorting Liberator bombers, even as he closed in to set a B-24 aflame.

Lieutenant S/G Baoshi Kanno, also of the Kanoya Wing, went down near Yaku Shima in the fight over Okinawa. An outstanding leader of other pilots against the B-29's, he was famous as the "bomber killer," with twelve victories over B-17 Flying Fortresses among his 52 confirmed air kills. Kanno was the Japanese pilot who originated the rolling-and-diving head-on attack against the B-17's, and perfected this technique—the most effective of all—against the B-29's.

These were the great pilots; too many of the remaining flyers lacked the training necessary to close effectively with the B-29's. Except for small, isolated fighter units spread throughout Japan, the fighter defense against the B-29's by the time Le May prepared for his great gamble was largely infective. The daylight defense was at best sporadic; lack of radar-equipped ground facilities and fighters led Le May to assume—and correctly—that the Japanese were without a worthwhile night-fighter defense.

Mustang

As for anti-aircraft guns, here the risk was essentially greater. Although the Japanese lacked the radar-sighting equipment which would increase their fire effectiveness, the B-29's were to come in at minimum altitude, thus exposing themselves to both the heavy anti-aircraft batteries and the automatic weapons normally used for lower altitude firing. And Tokyo, if nothing else, was a wasp's nest of guns.

How effective these guns might be against the B-29's brought down to "suicidal heights" would soon be proved.

10

GREEN FLARE

When the group briefings ended on the islands of Guam, Tinian, and Saipan, the planning phase of the most revolutionary of all B-29 strikes was almost complete. Now the crews broke up, talking quietly, and prepared for the more specific and demanding phase of the briefings—separate meetings for the airplane commanders, the flight engineers, radio operators, the radar teams of navigators and bombardiers.

For the first time there were no large groups of gunners, for the ground crews and armorers had been working overtime to strip the silvery bombers of their heavy turrets and the .50 caliber machine guns. Without the guns and the long belts of ammunition, the airplanes would be lighter, and Tokyo would feel the difference in the heavier load of bombs. It all worked out to a very specific formula; each B-29 normally carried an average load of 8,000 rounds of machine-gun shells. This added 3,200 pounds to the take-off load; translated into terms of effects upon Tokyo, this meant more than 500 M-69 incendiary bombs per airplane—or a total of *fifty thousand fire bombs* more from the fleet of raiders.

All told, more than two thousand tons of bombs were almost ready to cascade from the skies.

There was still some personal time left; the crews grabbed the opportunity to attend to last-minute details. Few men not assigned to the mission were "racking out," enjoying precious free time to sleep. It was a hot March afternoon in the Marianas; besides, the islands were by now buzzing with interest and anxiety. Those who were not flying either mingled with their flying mates or watched silently as the crews assigned to the missions went about their movements. Strangely enough, many of the gunners who had been scrubbed from the strike were busy driving their plane commanders crazy as they begged to go along—even if only to act as observers who would keep a lookout for other B-29's in the loose stream that would flow toward Japan.

In the barracks the men picked up their personal equipment, stuffed a book or a candy bar into the pocket of a flight jacket. Some of them wrote a last letter, sealed it, left it with a barracks mate "just in case." There was that strange feeling of going in without the guns, on the deck. They tried not to think of it, yet the thought remained as an undercurrent in back of their minds.

On the hardstands the ground crews were still at work, and would be until that last moment before the crews climbed aboard and the plane commanders were ready to start the great engines. There were crew chiefs still unsatisfied with the deep, throaty roar of the Wrights, and they ran the engines up into whining screams until everything sounded right, looked right, checked out right on the gauges.

Three hundred and thirty-four tremendous bombers, being prepared in an orchestral prelude for the flaming finale over Tokyo. The bomber crewmen rode on trucks to their hardstands, where the engines roared and the propellers whirled. High portable scaffolds reached up to the wings and the fuselage, and mechanics clambered up and down attending to last-moment requirements. They examined control surfaces, fuel lines, hydraulic lines, a thousand and one items. With their own peculiar set of mechanical-surgical instruments, they tightened and tested the nerves and tendons of the giants, observing on dials and gauges the reflexes of cables and pressure lines, assuring that the vital life fluids flowed as required through the slim metal veins and arteries.

A string of dollies led to each of the 334 planes, and one by one the dollies were rolled beneath the gaping twin

Hellcat

bomb bays in the belly of each Superfortress. A single strand of copper wire was looped under a bomb, and the wire itself attached to a lifting mechanism inside the plane which hoisted the package of clustered incendiaries into the capacious bay. As it lifted, the bomb teetered off balance on its wire; a calm hand steadied the deadly package, and finally the missile was latched properly into its place.

The crews in the meantime were busy. They had items to check; Mae Wests, oxygen masks, canteens, parachutes, survival equipment for bailing out or ditching at sea, flak vests, and other gear which might properly be marked: "How to Stay Alive."

Once in the airplanes, there were hundreds of additional items to inspect. In the wide, long nose the pilots and the flight engineer worked together running down a long checklist of several pages, going through dials, buttons, switches, gauges, controls. Behind them other equipment is inspected. There are oxygen flow regulators to test, hatches, power leads, ad infinitum. The navigators assemble their charts, slide rules, protractors, and other equipment.

Outside the airplanes, the mechanics perform their last chores before it is time to start engines. The final task is to "walk the props." Two men at a time grasp one of the four blades on each propeller and turn the prop around to flush excess oil from the engine.

Then it is time. Pilots and copilots and engineers flip switches to ON, turn magnetos to ON, check fuel flow, fuel pressure, the myriad items necessary to bring the giants to life. Sliding their cockpit windows back, the plane commanders look out and cry: "Clear on the left!"

The propellers turn laboriously, grinding around. Engines wheeze and groan, high-octane fuel sprays through the powerful Wrights. Engines catch, thunder grumbles outward, white smoke belches from the exhausts as the first notes of a crashing avalanche of sound begin.

On 334 hardstands, the mighty powerplants howl a song of power. The hardstands on each of the three islands are centers of activity; each has its ground crew watching with some anxiety as the propellers spin in blurs. Inside the Superfortress the crew checks carburetor temperatures and cowl-flap positions, fuel flow and pressure, tachometers for R.P.M., cylinder-head temperatures, oil pressure and temperature, radios and navigation equipment, radar—a thousand and one things to work in a coordination that almost defies the imagination.

"The story of a B-29 taking off," wrote an A.A.F. correspondent, "might well be a story of closing doors." The first doors to close are those in the twin bomb bays. At the command from his pilot, the flight engineer pushes a switch, and under the B-29 four metal doors swing up and join. It is what might be termed a ritual, for it is only at this moment that the bomber truly accepts its deadly cargo, seals it inside, and, unless there is some failure along the flight, commits itself to sowing its cargo of flaming destruction.

Then, with a rushing suddenness, all the minutes of waiting are gone. It is time to move out and jockey into position. The ponderous planes trundle along the ground, away from the hardstands.

Throttles move forward, power increases, blades whirl faster and faster, and the thunder becomes a pulsating roar. The sound rises and falls. In the midst of the crashing roar there comes the higher, unmistakable squeal of brakes, grabbing at the dual-wheels, as the heavy bombers are carefully maneuvered out onto the taxiways. The ground crews watch their machines trundle away; from the control tower other men watch. The cooks and clerks and guards and bakers and corpsmen and mechanics and hundreds more all stop what they are doing to watch.

The bombers move slowly into position, a groaning, elephantine procession, a parade of behemoths of the twentieth century. The Superfortresses shake the coral and the jungle growth and the Quonsets and the very air itself. It seems as though the very ground becomes fluid and quivers. The thunder rolls and booms and crashes and the two tidal waves from different lines of bombers meet; they rebound, leap and swirl, and then they assume a strange sort of resonance that results in an even greater buildup of sound. Sound and fury beyond the imagination.

White clouds of coral dust boil upward from the turbulence that whips away from the tips of propellers and slams into the earth, turbulence that can throw a man off his feet and toss him along like a tumbleweed.

The first planes move to the runway; on the flight

decks the pilots move the propeller controls forward into flat pitch, and the sound is murderous, a high, metallic scream of steel torturing air.

The pathfinders, first in line, swing from the taxiways to the active runway. In their twin bays are the napalm-filled M47 fire bombs, 180 missiles to each airplane. They will be the first in the air, the first to reach the enemy coast, the first to spill their flame into the sky to mark the heart of Tokyo with the signal for the planes behind them.

The first to be ready for takeoff are the B-29's of the 19th and 29th Groups of the 314th Wing. They are on Guam's North Field, and because Guam is farther down the island chain from Tokyo than either Tinian or Saipan, the 314th Wing planes will move out first. Forty minutes later the B-29's of the 73rd and 313th Wings will start to roll.

At ten seconds past 5:34 p.m. on March 9th, the first of the B-29's is on the runway. The pilot stares at the distant tower; suddenly he sees a brilliant white flare. Simultaneously, a flagman, standing no more than thirty feet from the whirling propeller blades, raises his hand.

Both signals mean the same thing—start rolling in ten seconds. The four throttles move forward in their grooves, the bomber strains with its nine thousand horsepower; it shakes and trembles, it wants to leap free of the restraining brakes. It is the din of demons.

A green flare bursts into the sky, shining, sputtering; the flagman's hand drops sharply.

The copilot of the first bomber cries out: *"Green light!"*

It means *"Go!"*

The first of the B-29's begins to roll down the long runway.

11

TARGET DEAD AHEAD

The B-29 weighs 138,000 pounds combat loaded, and it demands a lot of flying. Every takeoff is an exacting, nerve-teasing stretch of forty seconds that often seems like forty minutes. It is the longest leg of a mission that may run from twelve to fourteen hours. During those forty seconds every man is at razor-edge alertness, listening for a miss in the thundering beat of the four engines, for *anything* that may interfere with that ponderous acceleration down the long runway.

The 65-ton monster jerks forward when the pilot releases the brakes; the engines have been pounding under their maximum of 8,800 horsepower and they are eager to move, to bite into the air that swirls into and then back from the blades. She's heavy, loggy; despite the power, the rush is not wild. It is more stately, a mountain on wheels that by its own sheer mass resists movement—yet a mountain of wings and engines that was made to fly.

Finally she is fast enough for the wheels to spin into a blur and the tires to kick up streamers of dust. Acceleration increases with speed; it is a cycle that lends even more speed to the enormous machine as it rushes headlong toward the end of the runway—a point on the earth that approaches with alarming speed.

Now the airplane is moving too fast to stop. It must either fly or crash; the Superfortress is beyond the point of no return. The speed is past a hundred miles per hour, and the bomber rocks lightly on her wheels. The wings bite into the air, they try to grasp the viscous flow, but there is not yet enough speed. The B-29 wings are wide, but they are comparatively thin. Behind the wings drop enormous flaps; the airflow slamming into the flaps is altered in its movement, and lift increases. But it is not yet enough. If an engine falters now, disaster is certain, absolute—a flaming, exploding death for the men inside.

Sometimes it is not the engines that fail, but something else—unpredictable, unexpected. On this afternoon it does not happen, but every man in the bombers remembers one night. . . .

The B-29's were taking off at intervals of fifty seconds. One of the bombers raced down the 8,500-foot runway, gathering speed, with a tremendous rush. Then, suddenly, there appeared a thin stream of light, a pencil line of sparks that flashed suddenly from the main left gear. For some reason the brakes in that gear had locked, frozen, the wheels in place. The B-29 lacked the speed to get into the air, yet it was moving too swiftly to be stopped. If acceleration could have continued for only a few more seconds, flying speed would have been reached. But acceleration did not continue. In seconds friction heat turned the gear white-hot. Instantly the brake fluid in the lines began to burn. In another second the metal also burst into flame.

The sparks turned into a pyrotechnic stream. Suddenly, explosively, a tongue of pure white fire erupted from the gear and fled down the runway, trailing the stricken machine.

It all happened with frightening speed; yet to the men watching there was a strange slow-motion quality to it all. The wheels melted. In a swirling cloud of stinking, pungent vapor mixed with coral dust, the very rubber disappeared. As this occurred, the bomber began to settle to the left. In that second eleven men were condemned. On the flight deck the pilot and copilot jammed their feet with all their strength on the brake pedals, trying to stop a runaway monster. They chopped power, screamed in the interphone for the crew to brace themselves.

She began to slew to the left. The pressures on the

gear were fantastic. Suddenly the right gear strut, pulled and twisted by the slewing weight, collapsed. Men sucked in their breaths and watched with horror in their eyes.

She hit on her belly, a solid, sickening impact. The great frame that could absorb so much punishment in the air was not designed for impact with the earth. The body of the B-29 ruptured, split open along her belly like an animal gutted with a sweeping knife. The tanks split.

In the darkness the dust cloud boiling upward showed only briefly as the bomber ran crazily in an intense shower of sparks and burgeoning flame. The great airplane whipped off the runway, dashed herself into the jagged coral beyond.

There was an all-consuming, terrible flash of light. That was all.

But the B-29 was off the runway. That eleven were dead was a grievous, shocking, personal loss. What mattered at the moment was that the runway was clear. The green flare showed again, the hand came down, and another Superfortress trembled with power, and began its charge down the runway, with the pilot and copilot looking straight ahead and never once to where the flames licked at the shattered remnants of a sister ship. . . .

One after the other, on this bright sunlit afternoon of March 9th, the bombers rush away toward the end of the runway. The pilots nudge rudder pedals to keep their giants heading straight and true. There are some mechanical failures, but there are no accidents or disasters, and almost all of the 334 aircraft thunder into the sky.

In each airplane the copilot calls out in ten-mile-per-hour increments the increasing speed of the Superfortress. He sings out at 90, then 100 . . . 110 . . . 120 . . . 130 . . . 140 . . . 150. Still on the ground! Then the call of 160 miles per hour.

The pilot pulls easily, surely, but with a firm, experienced strength, on the control column in his hands. The column comes back, the nose wheel lifts off the runway. The angle of attack of the wings changes subtly, but it is enough. The air curves invisibly but with sudden new force around the wings, and lift increases sharply. At this moment the pilot waits—this is a moment when you can wait for hours in the time of only one second—to see if the balance is there, if lift exceeds gravity, and the wings with their enormous flaps have grasped solidly into the air.

The engines are too hot and there is a reef of coral ahead, razor-sharp, humpbacked, jagged. Through the plexiglas the crew looks out and watches the coral rush at them with frightening speed, but suddenly the wheels no longer are on the runway, they are inches above the blacktop; the giant is flying. In the cockpit the pilot's right thumb flashes upward, and the copilot hits the gear switch. The big struts and wheels fold upward neatly into their wells, the door covers shut, and the bomber is clean. Except for the flaps which still add lift; they will come up as speed begins to increase.

The moment of takeoff is but temporary relief. *Speed*—this is the most precious thing in the world right now. Speed must be built up. The Marianas air is hot and sticky, and the B-29 is sluggish and too heavy, not eager to fly.

With the airplane definitely airborne, the pilot nudges the control column forward. The nose drops gently. The bomber must be held straight and level to build up more speed.

The pilot flies with infinite caution. He cannot allow the nose to dip too far, or the Pacific will smash into the belly of the bomber. The pilot holds her down, milks the flaps up slowly. Some of the bombers are so close to the water that the churning wake flings spray into the air.

And then the pilot climbs, gently, carefully. Just a nudge on the column, but it is enough for the B-29 to respond, to put more distance between the silver belly and the water below. There is no turning or banking here, because the B-29 is a giant with wide wings and just a slight sideslip toward the water will mean a sudden tug, a cartwheel that will bring death and flaming explosion. But again, miraculously, it does not happen to a single B-29. In each airplane a dangerous adventure that has dragged out for forty terrible seconds is over; then the seconds of early flight. When the nose comes up gently and the ocean falls away before the eyes of the men, muscles relax and breathing is easier. Now there is only the problem of the long flight to Tokyo, and the flak and the fighters. But those are elements against which *something* can be done. Nothing is ever quite so helpless as that takeoff.

B-29's of the 19th and 29th Groups leave Guam; the first takeoff is officially noted in the control-tower log at 1735—35 minutes past 5 p.m. Forty minutes later, the bombers start from Guam and Saipan. It takes two hours and forty-five minutes for the entire force to become airborne; nearly three hours of crashing thunder, of those perilous forty-second trips down the runways.

The men in the flight decks trim out the bombers, turn for course, grateful that there is no need for assembly and the anxious watching carefully for the other airplanes which will slide into fuel-consuming patterns in the sky. The pilot makes his adjustments, and then turns his airplane over to the automatic flight control equipment, known as the "George" in airman's slang, an electronic piloting device that takes over flight. There is no rest at this point, of course, but the men are now busy attending normal tasks rather than sweating out the imminence of disaster.

As the airplanes climb, the flight engineer fusses over his controls. He has an absorbing interest in every pound, in every cupful of gasoline, because this means the difference on the way home of setting down on the very end of a runway for a successful landing, or dropping short into the coral at the end of the runway.

In the B-29 center section, known as C.F.C. (Central Fire Control), the men are for the first time in the history of B-29 operations without their normal duties. Tonight the turrets are empty, their powerful guns gone, and the blisters are being employed for a technique known as scanning. The bombers have no formation, they flow in a great, loose stream toward Tokyo, and the men who stare out the blisters are alert for other bombers.

In a niche stuck away in the left corner of the flight deck is the navigator. Tonight he feels an equality with other crew members that he hasn't known before. In the B-17 the navigator was also a gunner and could fire back at the German fighters, but the B-29 navigator has no gunnery station and can only stare out a tiny, square observation window and—just wait, and take it. But tonight, except for the tail gunner (and this is the last mission with those weapons in place), the entire crew can only "take it"—relying upon surprise and speed to elude the enemy defenses.

More than anyone else, because this is his world, the navigator knows how lonely the sea truly is; and his responsibility gains weight because everyone counts on him. He works with sharpened pencils, ruler, protractor and many charts; he checks assigned and emergency frequencies. He worries about winds—headwinds and tailwinds and quartering winds—and what they will do to speed in the air and over the surface of the earth; more important, what does all that mean in terms of target-time and landfall and the IP and fuel-against-miles to go home.

Tonight the navigators in all the B-29's look at a tiny dot marked Iwo Jima with feelings of good will and affection. In past months Iwo was a wasp's nest. It had fighters and flak and radar warning for the mainland; now, because many Marines have died and many more shed blood, the island is in American hands. It is a haven, an emergency landing field; it is also a friend along the "Hirohito Highway," because on Iwo there are great transmitters pulsing signals through space, a beam that will guide the B-29's onward to Tokyo and on the flight home.

Far forward, in the nose of the airplane, the bombardier hunches over his complicated equipment, stares through his plexiglas paneling as the world drifts by beneath him. His position is naked and exposed, and when the fighters come in and the flak crashes away, everything seems to point directly toward him. But he is the man who works the toggles and who can release the hell toward the enemy below; strangely, there is no personal vindiction. When the bombs are away there is only one emotion: "Let's get the hell out of here."

The official records of this mission state that on the flight to Tokyo the bombers "encountered turbulence and heavy cloud." Because there were no formations with their restrictions on flight, the weather imposed less than the usual hardships on the B-29's. As they rumbled toward Japan, the sky was mostly clear. Darkness comes slowly over the infinite expanse of the Pacific, and the new moon shows itself weakly in the sky, little more than a pale silvery arc. Yet there is still light: from the stars, from the very glow of the night air. The bombers stay low, and only the shadows flitting through the flight deck give proof of the clouds overhead.

The clouds become thicker, and soon the bombers are in the midst of the infamous weather lying between Saipan and the Japanese mainland. The air is alive with currents and sweeping gales, and the B-29's shake and vibrate and bounce. The crews strap themselves in, stoically ignoring the weather with which they are so familiar, and wait for Japan to come closer.

But this is the time for caution, and every eye is at a window or a blister, staring out for the telltale lights sliding through the blackness—the navigation lights of the other bombers. There are no fighters out here, no flak, no observers, and the lights are essential to prevent a shattering collision high over the Pacific.

Tokyo comes closer and closer, and the men stir to action. They begin to don their armor, twentieth-century coats of mail. They put on flak suits—heavy, bulky, uncomfortable. But the suits do a terrific job in stopping those pieces of shrapnel, hot and jagged, from ripping into a man's body. They put on heavy steel helmets. They are like infantrymen in some strange, winged creature surging through the skies.

Now, as the target draws closer the flight engineers are checking fuel consumption, flow, pressure, cylinder-head temperatures, RPM, and speed and altitude—a thousand things to be absolutely certain that the great, complicated mass of machinery is functioning perfectly as it rushes to do battle.

In the blunted nose of the B-29, staring through the panels, the land and the nation still invisible in the night become revealed. Not by direct sight, but because there is a glow, a faint pulsation on the horizon.

On the radar set, the land mass begins to creep along the glowing face. Landfall is made with precision, but it is almost unnecessary to watch the scope or even to look for the land mass as it becomes visible. The pathfinders have struck, and with deadly accuracy.

Far ahead a flame has been kindled in the heart of a city, and the pilot officially alerts his crew with the words that bring every man up a little straighter, the words that mean commitment to battle: *"Target dead ahead."*

Time has run its course with Tokyo. Thousands of feet below, still far ahead of most of the bomber mass in the night skies, the first people are already dying under the terrible caress of flames.

12

THE FLAMING X

The pathfinders rushed in first, well ahead of the first massed wave of the bomber stream, their striking time coordinated down to the last second. Over an area of Tokyo with 103,000 persons to the square mile, one of the most congested spots of the world, the lead B-29's raced in at less than five thousand feet. Engines wide open, diving slightly to bring their speed to well over 300 miles per hour, they sped over Tokyo with almost total surprise.

The 100-pound, M47A2 napalm bombs worked with devastating success. It was what the crews called a good bombing night. The skies were clear with scattered clouds; initially the visibility was better than ten miles, and the cloud cover never reached more than three-tenths.

Into the designated target area of ten square miles poured the clusters of pathfinder bombs. At a hundred feet over the city the 500-pounders split open, shredding the napalm bombs outward. These scattered, and the napalm blazed immediately upon contact, feeding hungrily upon the flimsy walls and rooftops where they struck.

The first two airplanes streaked across the city, nearly two hundred bombs showering downward along their high-speed runs. First one B-29 laid a blazing swath along its target path; immediately after, the second plane dashed in, crossing the line of falling bombs.

The napalm is an insidious, sticky incendiary, and it sows fire on contact, sets aflame its objectives in less than a second. The first Japanese searchlights were stabbing the sky as the pathfinders fled.

Behind them they left a wide, perfect flaming X, directly in the heart of the target area. That blazing X was all that was needed.

The message flashed back to XXI Bomber Command Headquarters—*"Bombing the target visually. Large fires observed. Flak moderate. Fighter opposition nil."*

The first bombs fell at exactly fifteen minutes after midnight. There was a brisk wind blowing in Tokyo, and in seconds the situation was disastrous. The flame grasped at the wood-bamboo-plaster construction, and leaped with explosive fury from wall to wall, from roof to roof. Within thirty minutes—by a quarter of one—as the fire chief of Tokyo was to report later, the situation "was completely out of control; we were absolutely helpless."

Following the first two pathfinders came ten more of the giant B-29s. They dumped their bombs into the area marked by the blazing X carved out in the heart of the Tokyo slums. Behind them came an armada that was to pour fiery hell into Tokyo for three hours of continuous attack.

Millions of the deadly incendiary bombs rained from the sky into Tokyo. In the city, fear mounted to stark terror. The pilots of the early planes reported that Tokyo was illuminated like a forest of brightly lighted Christmas trees. The flames were still separate, but beginning to spread. They were thousands and thousands of tiny flickering candles. But they grew, and they merged.

In the beginning, the crews commented with interest on the scene. The last planes brought men into something entirely different. It was the maw of hell; like flying over a super-blast furnace that shrieked and roared with its insane fires.

Several miles outside of the attacked area stood the house of a member of the Swedish legation. Fascinated and horrified, he watched the entire scene develop right before his eyes. Later, when it was all over and the shock of the fantastic sight had subdued, he said: "It seems to me when I think of it now that the B-29's started to come in like a fan, coming in from two sides, very low. The fan seemed to come to a point right over my house. The bombers were beautiful. Their colors changed like chameleons. They were greenish as they passed through the searchlights, and red as they flew over the glare of the fire. At first the anti-aircraft fire was rather strong but seemed badly aimed. Later, as the fires grew worse, it died away. I saw one plane being shot down, falling in several pieces. An intense fire broke out where it fell. Another developed a huge golden, glowing bowl underneath it—I expect one of the incendiaries had exploded inside—and limped off over the horizon.

"The flames were very colorful. The white buildings of brick and stone were burning, and they gave off a very deep color. The wooden houses gave off a light yellow flame, and a huge billow of smoke hung over the edge of the bay."

The Japanese who stared in fright and terror at the wind-whipped flames bearing down upon them saw no beauty nor any pattern developing from the screaming fires. The wind shifted and roared, and quickly shot to hurricane force, bearing down upon tens of thousands of people with the speed of an express train.

But before we move deeply into Tokyo, into the heart of the single most devastating fire the human race has ever known, let us return to the waves of bombers in their loose stream, as they approach the city in which the great, flaming X has been burned. It is a scene that few men have ever witnessed; and those who saw it from the sky, the executioners, have stated that they hope that never again will they, or other men, ever be forced to look straight into the very heart of hell.

The first sight of Japan is a faint, barely seen pink glow on the distant horizon. It is at first no more than a flickering touch of luminescence; you would not know that a city is burning. The visibility is ten miles; seen from a greater distance, the glow is fuzzy and indistinct, more of a blur than truly a light.

But the great bombers rush at nearly three hundred miles per hour toward the capital of Japan, and the miles flee quickly. The glow increases in size, becomes brighter.

Now the mountains of Japan are distinct against the sky; the ridges are black and silhouetted, but familiar to the veteran crews. In the nose of the bombers, over the greenish glow of the instrument panels, the pilots and co-pilots, the bombardiers and the navigators, the flight engineers—they all stare out. They have been over Japan before, they have sown explosive and incendiary bombs.

But they have never seen the heart of a city being gouged out of existence by flame.

Tokyo rushes closer, and soon the light is reflected on the glass of the bomber noses, it shines off the leading edges of the wings, glints off the propellers. Then the haziness of the light has vanished, and the men see clearly the intense white spears of the larger fires, spawn of the original napalm, whipped to insane frenzy by the M-69 missiles. Magnesium burns in air; it blazes with an intolerable white light, and in those areas where the greater flames have not yet reached, there can be seen the intense pinpoints of light. Here the B-29's have unleashed thousands of bombs that are just starting to burn.

Each Superfortress rushed in with twenty-four 500-pound bombs, and each of these 500-pounders released a cluster of the magnesium incendiaries. In the pathfinders the intervalometers were set to release the napalm bombs at 100-foot intervals; the main stream of raiders had theirs set for fifty feet. It was very precise, very carefully planned. On this basis the attacked area was receiving a minimum density of twenty-five tons—8,333 magnesium bombs—per square mile!

The stream of bombers attacked an area of rectangular shape, roughly four by three miles. But so rapidly did the flames spread, that the bombardiers were able to follow their orders to fan out and hit those areas as yet unbombed. Thus fires were created over a much greater area than had been anticipated. It is terrible to contemplate the effect of fire in areas with a population density of 103,000 persons per square mile; the Japanese realized immediately, however, that the casualties would be beyond belief when a long stream of B-29's concentrated on the Asakusa Ward

—where there were nearly 140,000 people to the square mile, and a building density exceeding 50 percent!*

The bombers rush in, the crews stare, many of them unable to speak of the holocaust raging below. There are clouds in the sky, but even at some distance from Tokyo, the clouds passing beneath the airplanes do not block out the light that expands and swells with every passing second.

Nor is there only light; there is heat. The fire is a thing alive now. It dances and writhes on the ground, back of the waters of Tokyo Bay; it swells monstrously as the men stare with mixed horror and fascination.

When they look up at the higher layer of clouds there is still light. The sky changes. The angry red that boils and seethes on the ground vanishes at these heights; it is an unbelievably beautiful pink, a soft illumination that suffuses the bottoms of the higher clouds, that turns the heavens into a vast amphitheater of light that at any other time *would* be beautiful.

There is light in the skies over Tokyo from sources other than the flames. The Japanese are defending their city. They have been caught unawares and they are stunned by the catastrophe unfolding before them; they see the flames advancing toward their gun positions, but until the flames wash over the guns, or the heat sets their clothes afire, the gunners remain at their positions, blasting away. They have little radar, and what they do have is almost useless. Searchlights stab the sky, but they are not needed. The great bombers are clearly outlined by the dancing flames; they form a long river in the skies, unreal shapes rushing overhead, their thunder nearly drowned out by the crashing of the flames.

Seen from a distance at night, flak is unreal. If it were not deadly, it would be lovely. Tiny sparks appear in the sky as if by magic; they wink into being, and subside almost immediately, soundless, shapeless. These are the heavy shells exploding. Sometimes, out of the angry, flam-

*The Bronx in New York City, filled with high tenements, has a population density of only 34,000 people per square mile. San Francisco's population density is 14,250 per square mile. Even the *center* of Hiroshima, as of August 1st, 1945, had only 35,000 per square mile.

ing carnage on the ground, brighter sparks appear, red and yellow; these ascend slowly into the heavens in long red streaks. They are rockets, new defenses for Tokyo, blazing shells that trace strange arcs upward from the tortured earth.

There are also curving, twisting necklaces of glowing lights; tracer shells from the smaller guns. The Japanese are firing frantically, hysterically, pumping shells and bullets into the air as fast as their overheated guns will allow. In the midst of all this blazing reception, a different white appears; a soft and diffused glow of white that sends streamers out in all directions—smoking tendrils. These are the arms and the fingers of phosphorous shells hurled into the air by Japanese defenses.

Sometimes the shells strike, and a great, flaming fireball plummets from the heavens to mark the death of a bomber and the men within. But even this success has its own curse, for every Superfortress brought down is a bomb weighing sixty tons, filled with metal and magnesium and oil and thousands of gallons of high-octane fuel. Each bomber that crashes—though they are few—is certain to wipe out not one, but several huge blocks, and to kill hundreds of hapless Japenese who have time only to look up and see the meteoric mass plunging down upon them before the world blots out in a stabbing knife of red.

The study of Tokyo during the approach is brief, for the bombers close in rapidly to the IP (Initial Point), where they will turn and then rush for their bombing strikes. As they approach the IP there comes the first change in power; pilots shove the four throttles all the way forward and the engines answer back with a richer, huskier roar. At the same moment the pilots cry *Props!* to the men at their right; the co-pilots push forward on the propeller controls, the blades turn and go into flatter pitch, and the propellers throw off their knife-edged, keening, metallic sound. The bombers gain in power and in speed.

The B-29's climb above their assigned bombing altitudes. The pilots have been briefed to maintain a certain speed during the bomb run, but this is impossible with the heavy load of bombs and the still-heavy load of fuel aboard. So the Superfortresses come into their positions for the IP with every ounce of power in their great engines; the speed gain is slight, but not the power, and the thrashing propellers drag the bombers to greater heights.

The navigator chants into the interphone, counting down the seconds to the IP, where the pilot will turn for the run over the blazing target. "Four—three—two—one— start your turn now. . . ."

Now the IP is behind the airplane, and the B-29 is committed to the test of fire. The pilot pushes forward on the control column and there comes another change in sound, meaningful to the experienced. The nose goes down, the labored rhythm of the engines eases as the propellers spin faster. The giant airplane is moving downhill now, and she runs before her power, weight, and gravity and drops out of the sky in the long, slanting race. Then there is all the speed that the pilot needs, and the control column inches back.

A new sound comes; subdued, but meaningful to the men aboard the airplanes. It is a change in the sound of wind. The bombardier coordinates with his pilot, and a switch has been closed. Four doors are open now, exposing the hellish cargo carried in the two great bays.

With a peal of thunder the bombers rush toward downtown Tokyo. What had first been a distant glow, is now a shifting, writhing mass on the earth. Tokyo does not exist; at least not the heart of the city. The earth itself has been torn away by a great blade of burning steel. There is left a jagged tear, a massive, gaping fissure in the earth itself. It pulses with fire like a live creature. Separated from the people below by several thousand feet of superheated air, the bomber crews see the streets only as avenues and rivers of fire. People burn, their skin peeled suddenly like grapes thrown into a furnace, but all of this is hidden from the air.

Even at this instant a living wall of flame sweeps through Tokyo. Not a pillar of fire, or a great mass of flame, but literally a tidal wave of flame that advanced over the earth, devouring everything combustible in its path. It leaves behind it embers and lesser fires, total death and ashes and the remnants of terror in the form of bodies charred and pulverized by heat that cannot be believed.

From the air this wall of fire is not sharp and defined, but yet it is visible. The men in the bombers look down and do not believe what they see. The base of the wave is streaked with white; the intense, impossible white that comes from an arc lamp, or the heart of a pressure-fed, white-hot blast furnace. The city is an ocean, a great churning mass burning and writhing in its own cremation.

But there is no end to it. The radarmen in the B-29's stare into their scopes and shout to the bombardiers, "Drop 'em! Drop your bombs! The scope is blank—drop 'em *now*!"

And another seven tons of hell spill into the city, cascading earthward to feed the creature below that is consuming Tokyo with its ravenous, unquenchable thirst of fire.

13

WALL OF FIRE

What began in Tokyo at fifteen minutes past midnight was an incipient firestorm. This was the same kind of towering flame that had consumed the heart of the German city of Hamburg and other great urban centers in the Reich. All the conditions were ripe in Tokyo for the greatest blaze ever known: building density and the inflammability of the target area promised a firestorm reaching to fifteen or twenty thousand feet above the earth.

The concentration of bombs per square mile—and in a period of only a few hours—exceeded in severity the attack on Hamburg by the Royal Air Force. But there was no firestorm—and all because of a wind.

Assuming combustibility and building density, a firestorm requires the creation of tens of thousands of individual fires within a limited area and in a short period of time. In merging, these fires create immediately a cyclonic effect, as do all large fires.

In the absence of a prevailing ground wind, the fires rapidly merge into great central blazes, all drawing in air from the perimeter of their flames. The suction of these flames overcomes natural prevailing weather; the several great fires join into a single blaze that is known as the firestorm. In Hamburg this fire reached fantastic proportions, producing heat on the periphery of the fire of 1,472 degrees Fahrenheit and winds of hurricane force. Everything within the firestorm was utterly consumed; if it could burn, it burned. If it could not burn, it often melted. Any living creature trapped within the periphery of the fire-storm was doomed.

Within ten to twenty minutes after the original flaming X was carved into the heart of downtown Tokyo, conditions were even more favorable for a firestorm than they had been in Hamburg in July of 1943, with the one exception of an existing surface wind at the moment the fires began to leap upward.

At this period in the attack, nature itself decided the outcome of the flames. Without that wind, an enormous pillar of fire would have leaped into existence. Because of the wind, the potential firestorm was transformed at once into an even deadlier force—*the sweep conflagration*.

Just as Hamburg in July of 1943 became the first city in history ever to know the firestorm, so Tokyo in March of 1945 became the world's first city ever to suffer the sweep conflagration. A technical term, sweep conflagration means something quite different from "a large fire blazing out of control." What leaped into being in Tokyo was literally a tidal wave of flame.

As the fires ignited by the initial attack flashed through the inflammable Japanese homes, they shot almost instantly high above the buildings. The spread of fire was beyond belief; it was like a great forest fire blazing in dry timber. Under these conditions fire does not simply spread, it *explodes* as it moves along. It gathers itself into great blazing spheres and like a living creature leaps from building to building, shoots across hundreds of feet, and smothers its objective in a great searing flash that in an instant transforms an entire block, or group of blocks, into an inferno.

Whipped by 28 mile-per-hour surface winds, the fires spread rapidly to leeward. But as they did so, they merged with new fires already started, pools of flame and heat and suction from the tens of thousands of magnesium bombs blazing fiercely, unchecked, ignored by the Japanese who fled for their lives.

The tidal wave began to gather its strength.

A pillar of flame appeared, grew to a solid wall of fire

leaping high above the blazing rooftops. Then it bowed to the increasing force of the wind, and began to bend.

It bent more and more toward the ground, like the curving lip of a great breaker about to smash itself against a rocky shore. Only the breaker is alive, an enormous, thundering comber of flame. The higher the wind, the more the pillar leans over.

The more it leans over, the closer the flaming gases and searing radiated heat came to the combustible materials on the ground. And, the closer the pillar—extending rapidly on each side—comes to the ground, the richer the content of the oxygen it burns. Correspondingly, its temperature is higher. In Tokyo on this night, it exceeded the fantastic level of 1,800 degrees Fahrenheit!

The chief characteristic of this sweep conflagration, to approach it in a clinical sense, is the presence of a massed fire front, an extended wall of fire that moves to leeward, preceded by a mass of preheated vapors so hot that it can bring unconsciousness and even death to the victims caught in its path.

This is what was happening below the B-29's as they came in over Tokyo, at altitudes extending from 4,200 feet to 9,000 feet.

Below them, everywhere, incredible agony stalked the blazing streets. People were dying, roasting alive, by the thousands. But it could not be seen or felt from the air. There were the slashing flames and the fantastic mixtures of color—white and orange and crimson—the great masses of superheated, flaming gases that shot ahead of the fire wall like the jet from a gigantic furnace. There were great boiling clouds of smoke that thundered upward from the flaming carnage, smoke that momentarily obscured from view the fire, but could never hide the deep, angry, glowing, fearful red. It was as though the men looked down upon the surface of a planet still in its throes of creation, still lashed and whipped by vast and terrible volcanic fury.

There was fear in Tokyo below the airplanes, and also hate. Many a Japanese gunner died at his post, screaming hate and pumping shells futilely into the air, until a blast of superheated air exploded his clothes and hair and body into flames.

Until the guns were overrun by heat or flame, Tokyo showed its defiance. Tracers and shells and rockets spat into the air. The guns fired until the barrels turned white hot and began to melt. No less than forty-two of the great raiders were hit; these flew home to show their scars to the men on Saipan or Guam, or perhaps Iwo or Tinian.

Nine of the great bombers fell into the city of Tokyo, to contribute by their very death to the savage flames. Another five, crippled but flyable, managed to stagger away from Tokyo, to reach out to the south to the ocean, finally to ditch on the water. All five crews were saved.

The men in the bombers had never known anything like what was happening to them. The skies over Tokyo became a sea of absolute violence, a vast devil's cauldron boiling and raging. Tremendous blows smashed at the wings and the bodies of the Superfortresses. Waves of heat danced and shimmered visibly.

The thermals that soared upward from Tokyo were too much to believe. Sixty-ton bombers were flung about like matchsticks; B-29's at five thousand feet were thrust upward in a few seconds to eight or nine thousand feet. More than likely these thermal forces were as important as the anti-aircraft fire in downing several of the bombers. If a pilot attempted to hold his bombing altitude against the violent vertical columns of superheated air, he would exceed the structural limitations of his plane. It was as if he had shoved the control column all the way forward and dived the airplane at great speed until the wings collapsed.

The thermals spread out four miles laterally from the center of the fire. Japanese fighter pilots in the air over Tokyo reported they were unable to control their light airplanes, that they were flung helplessly around the sky and could not swing into pursuit curves to attack the racing B-29's.

"Gusts from the inferno were so powerful," wrote one sergeant, "that the men were rattled around inside the ships like dice in a cup. Floor boards were uprooted. All loose equipment was hurled about like shrapnel. More than one man was hurt that night because of those violent thermals."

B-29's at six thousand feet were caught by the shattering force of the superheated air, and flipped upside down, onto their backs. Often the planes fell several thousand feet before the shaken pilots could recover.

One bomber was caught in a particularly severe rising column of superheated air. Without warning the heavy airplane shot skyward, the pilot helpless at the controls. Within several seconds the airplane was flung from seven thousand to more than twelve thousand feet; the nose flashed upward, went straight up, and in those few seconds the B-29 was inverted at nearly two and a half miles above the city. By some miracle, the Superfortress completed its maneuver with the crew and all loose gear against the ceiling, fell down and back in a screaming loop, and streaked earthward. With both the pilot and copilot straining with all their might the airplane came out of its wild plunge only two hundred feet over Tokyo Bay. Wings bent sharply upward from the terrible strain, the B-29 leveled out at nearly 450 miles per hour and went howling out of range of the shore guns before the astonished Japanese could react.

The men in the early waves reported that, from a mile and a half above, the city looked like a vast bed of red-hot and burned-out embers. Those who flew over Tokyo in the final waves said they could almost hear the city screaming in its agony. The streets were barely visible in the midst of the sea of flames. Along the fire front the fire was a blinding white. Where the great tidal wave had passed whole city blocks glowed a dark red.

In many parts of the city even the dark lines of streets had vanished, spattered with strange flickering lights. These were burning trees and telephone poles, the fires getting the contents of a fireproof building, the scorched shell of a truck or a trolley car. Buildings had collapsed into the streets, gas lines flamed. Tokyo had become a slag heap, a garish wasteland of still-burning wreckage.

But above all else, there was one thing which brought home vividly what was happening down there in one of the world's greatest cities.

Because of the low altitudes of the mission, the B-29's remained unpressurized. The men did not need to wear their oxygen masks.

Inside the airplanes, the fumes swept in from the city.

A mist began to fill the cabins; a strange mist, blood-red in color.

The men could not bear what that mist brought with it.

Choking, spluttering, coughing—many of them vomiting forcefully—they grabbed their masks, slapped the rubber to their faces, drank in gratefully of the clean oxygen.

They could take everything else. But not the overpowering, sweet-sick stench of the burning flesh that permeated the skies two miles over the tortured city.

14

THE BURNING STREETS

This is the story of people in Tokyo who suffered the great incendiary attack on March 9-10, 1945. It is the story of the "little people," who are so rarely identified. They are like the people everywhere who were on the receiving end of the bombs. Here are a few who are not nameless.

It is one hour before midnight on March 9th. In the downtown section of Tokyo the sirens atop the public buildings are screaming their mournful, sometimes shrill, warning. This is a familiar sound by now in Tokyo, but a siren is a terrible thing to hear. Almost every home in the city has a radio, and the inhabitants listen with infinite care. They do not often turn on these sets; it is impossible to obtain replacement parts. When a tube flickers and dies out, there are no new tubes. The radio is used only on special occasions—like this one, when the Americans are coming in their enormous bombers, the great silver B-29's.

Yet the people are not excited. There is no hysteria, no panic in the narrow side streets or the broad avenues. Week after week, for months the sirens have wailed across the rooftops of Tokyo. The people are accustomed to the sound. They have heard it so many times when no American bombers came that the wail of sirens is a normal part of life.

From the way the sirens sound now, at eleven P.M., it is clear that this is not a warning of attack. The sirens' warning is for *Keikai Keiho*—the Standby Alarm. There is no cause for excitement, no cause for worry.

The *Keikai Keiho* is simply a requirement of wartime life. When even one enemy airplane is sighted near the coastline of Japan, the defense authorities order the Standby Alarm to be sounded.

Only if they hear the *Kushu Keiho* will the people react. For that is the warning that means *Air Raid!* And in order not to interfere with production in the factories, *Kushu Keiho* is heard only when the enemy airplanes are within fifty miles.

The radios sputter suddenly as all stations are switched to a single broadcasting studio. "Attention! Attention! Here is information from Eastern Headquarters. Standby alarms have been sounded because a group of enemy bombers have been reported circling over Choshi. There is no immediate danger. . . ."

Choshi is a fishing port more than fifty miles to the east of Tokyo. It is used often by the big American airplanes as a landmark. As has happened many times before, it is likely that the bombers will go to some place other than Tokyo.

These are the thoughts of Mrs. Kikue Mizuta, an attractive twenty-four year old Japanese woman. They are comforting thoughts, and in relief she strokes the brow of her sleeping son, Makoto, who is five years old. Six months earlier Mrs. Mizuta's husband was drafted into the Navy.

The house has been quiet since Mr. Mizuta's departure. There must be a terrible need for men in the Navy, for the Mizuta home is also a small workshop. Before the war the Mizuta family made umbrellas. Since 1941, however, they have made parts for machine guns. But the elder parents are too feeble to operate the complicated machinery. It lies unused beneath its cover.

The announcer's voice dies away, and recorded music comes from the radio. It is a serenade, almost as if the defense authorities were telling the people not to worry about the bombers, to go to bed, or return to work, if this is their shift. Mrs. Mizuta slips beneath a blanket on the floor near her sleeping son.

Two blocks away, in another house, Hisashi Tsukakoshi, who is twenty-seven years old, is sitting up in his bed. He is unhappy, for he fears that the radio will disturb his child, who is only fifteen days old. Mrs. Tsukakoshi, twenty-one years old, is very tired from a difficult birth.

The announcer comes on again, but only to reassure everyone that the bombers are still circling Choshi. Then the music resumes.

Mr. Tsukakoshi's home is also a small workshop. Once the machines produced parts for automobiles. Now Mr. Tsukakoshi manufactures filters for the lubrication oil systems of bombers and fighters. Five women work in the shop. They left two hours before their working time was over; parts are so short that there is nothing to keep them busy.

Another twenty minutes pass. Mr. Tsukakoshi is still wide awake. He cannot sleep; he has a premonition that everything is not well. It is a sixth sense; it disturbs him. He glances at his wife and child, rises in the darkness, and climbs the stairway to the roof.

The night is dark, and in all directions around him Tokyo is completely blacked out. Mr. Tsukakoshi suddenly sucks in his breath, fear striking at his heart. There is an airplane in the sky! He concentrates on the dark shape. Is it Japanese, or could it be an American bomber? There is no warning yet, the sirens have not sounded again, but a cold chill sweeps through Mr. Tsukakoshi.

For in this moment he makes out all too clearly the four engines of the airplane. He has seen the B-29 before, but always many miles above the city. This bomber is in a shallow dive, and it is moving faster than he has ever seen a B-29 fly before. It is like an evil black creature swooping out of the darkness.

Strangely, he cannot hear the sound of the engines. But he does not ponder this matter, for he can make out against the very dim light of the night sky a series of black specks. They have come from the B-29, and even as he watches the specks fall rapidly toward the city. Mr. Tsukakoshi stares with total absorption. He is not concerned for his own safety, or that of his family. Whatever is falling from the sky will land more than a mile away, and his house is in no danger.

The seconds pass so slowly as the specks fall!

Then, strangely, there is a light in the sky—well above the rooftops. The black things that were falling have suddenly broken apart. Fire leaps outward in several directions. Mr. Tsukakoshi watches the eerie flames falling downward, scattering in many different directions.

Where they land, there is a dim glow. Then, no more than a minute or two later, flames shoot up across a large area. Flames from burning buildings, leaping rapidly above the city roofline.

He looks around and his eyes widen in disbelief. He has heard only the first bomber as it came by him. But flames are spurting into the sky from all directions! He turns around and around, and almost before his eyes he watches the fire licking hungrily at rooftops, leaping up walls.

He suffers a moment of panic, but forces himself to think clearly. There are hundreds of small fires already, but they are far away. They are at least two to four miles in the distance.

But all Japanese have a deep mistrust of fire. If flames come near his house, what will happen? the thought appalls Mr. Tsukakoshi, for he has read many books, and heard his parents speak of the terrible earthquake and the fire of 1923, when flames roared right through the same area where his house stands.

He studies the sky more intently—there! Another bomber! And again the great machine swoops down toward Tokyo, the specks fall earthward, and again the specks scatter in mid-air, the fire blossoms in the air over the rooftops, and then disappears as it falls into the buildings.

This is too much for the young man. Fear gives wings to his feet, he dashes madly down the stairs, shouting: "Father! Mother! Yoshiko! Get up, get up, quickly! We're being attacked! The B-29's are over the city. Go to where it is safe; *hurry!* I will be there right after you!"

The Tsukakoshi family flees at the bidding of the young husband.

Three blocks from the Tsukakoshi home, Senko Hayashi lives with her aged parents. Their living quarters are behind a small store along the main street of Ishiwara, the center of Shitamachi; they deal in kitchen utensils.

At the time the Tsukakoshi family is fleeing to a safer haven, Semko Hayashi has dashed to the street to see what is happening. Ishiwara is fifty yards wide, and now it is filled with people who have rushed from their bedrooms to see what is happening. They stand around, uneasy, not sure of what to do. The *Kushu Keiho* has not sounded, there have been no explosions. What is everyone so excited about? What is happening?

Something must be wrong with the alarm system. Three men are running down the center of the street, two voluntary firemen and a policeman. They shout to everyone near them as they run: "It is an attack! It is an incendiary attack! All children and the old people must go immediately to the Futaba Primary School! Stay there until the bombers have gone! Hurry, hurry!"

Suddenly, something drops in the center of the wide avenue. It is a small black tube about two feet long. The people step back instinctively, then rush away. For a tremendous flame bursts from the small object! There is nothing that can burn near the black shape, but it continues to blaze. The people stare in fright, muttering to themselves. The fire is intense, it burns fiercely, giving off a strange odor that reminds Senko Hayashi of the cheap lubricating oil she uses for her bicycle.

She remembers that at this moment she felt a cold hand clutch at her heart. She has never heard of a thing two feet long that burns in this fashion, that lights up the whole street. What if it had landed among the houses?

And then she, and everyone else, hears the sound of motors. Many, many motors. A sound of deep thunder coming from the sky. Searchlights appear suddenly, and then they hear the cracking sounds of the anti-aircraft guns. They can see the white flashes in the sky. Someone shouts and points—there! The B-29's. But they are so low! And from their bellies there are hundreds of the small shapes!

Senko Hayashi is twenty-six years old, a widow. She was married at twenty and six months later her husband died from typhoid fever. Since then she has worked as a clerk at the Board of Fisheries. She has not remarried. Because she is the lone heir of the Hayashi family, it is not easy for her to discover a man who will come to live in her home, as an "adopted son" of her parents, in accordance with the Japanese family system. Her family is old; her father is sixty-seven and her mother fifty-six.

She looks at the sky, and shudders from the cold chill that she feels. "Father, Mother—go quickly," she says. "Go at once to the school building. They have a large swimming pool there. It will be much safer for you. I will be along right away."

Her parents nod assent and leave; Senko rushes back into the house. She does not know that this is the last time she will ever see her mother and father.

Inside the house Senko closes tightly the stone entrance to the basement where the family has stored some precious foodstuffs. Then she opens the safe, takes out the family's securities and wraps these around her waist, beneath her kimono. She has been prepared for moments such as these; she tightens her *Mompei* (kimono trousers), grasps a knapsack with family valuables and treasured mementos, and slings it to her shoulder. There are no steel helmets for ordinary civilians, so she puts on a deep cap made in the style of a fireman's hat.

Senko feels that she has not been in the house longer than ten minutes. But when she rushes outside again she stops in horror. At this moment she hears the cracking roar of the bombers overhead, the crash of the anti-aircraft shells. But what strikes fear to paralyze her legs is a wall of flame bearing down upon the very spot where she stands!

She can hear the crackling and roaring of the fires. The street is wild chaos, a bedlam of hundreds of shrieking, hysterical people, fleeing before the advancing fires. She cannot believe her eyes; she has been inside for only ten minutes!

How is all this possible? Has the world gone mad?

Then she notices the wind. Strong gusts blow down

the street. The air, even as she watches, begins to fill with sparks and firebrands. It is like the beginning of a snow-storm, the first minutes of a heavy snowfall. But now the flakes are alive and burning, an angry red.

It was stupid to remain in this place. Senko turns with the crowd and begins to run with them, away from the ad-vancing flames.

All this time no one has seen a fire engine, or any fire-men, except the two volunteers who shouted the warning to flee. It is a terrible thing to realize, but Shitamachi, so vul-nerable to fire, containing as it does the four wards of Honjo and Fukugawa on the eastern side of the river and Asakusa and Nihonbashi on the western side, has almost no defense against flames. In the Honjo ward, where the Hayashi, Tsukakoshi, and Mizuta families live, there are only four fire brigades. Against the B-29 incendiary attack, they are overwhelmed and totally useless right from the start of the bombing.

In the Honjo ward there are fifty school buildings; in Fukugawa fifty-one. All of these buildings are shelters, so designated by the authorities.

Of these schools, Futaba and three others are famous for their large swimming pools. This is a natural haven to people fleeing fire. Many thousands of people flock to these schools. There is no way to tell that the school build-ings lie in the path of the terrible wall of flame which at that very moment is starting its march across the city.

Every one of the more than thirteen thousand people who jam into the schools for safety from the flames will burn to death.

For the moment, let us leave the families of Hayashi, Tsukakoshi, and Mizuta; we shall come back to them presently.

Near the southern end of the Shitamachi area lives Mrs. Momoko Nagamine, thirty-six years old, and her daughter Toshie, aged fifteen. The home of Mr. Nagamine, who is a teacher of flower arrangements and tea cere-monies, is about two miles north of the people we have met so far. The house is at Mukojima, and is five hundred yards from the Sumida River. Mrs. Nagamine is a widow.

On this night there are visitors in the house. Mrs.

Nagamine's brother-in-law, Minetaro Nagamine, forty-seven years old, is a grocery-store owner; he, his three children and one maidservant, are staying at the house. They have been here since the previous month, when the B-29 attack of February 25th burned their home to the ground in the area of Minami Senju, about one mile west of the Mukojima area where they are now staying.

Minetaro Nagamine is a hardened veteran of fire disasters. In 1921 a fire burned his house out. Two years later there came the great earthquake, and his house collapsed and then exploded in flame. Now he has lost his third home to the B-29's.

When the sirens finally sound the alarm, Minetaro sees the first flames from the roof, where he has gone to watch. He dashes back into the house. "Everybody put on some clothes and get ready to leave at once!'" he shouts.

His sister-in-law protests. "Why must we leave?" she asks. "Why can't we just go to the school that is near the house?"

Minetaro roars in anger. "Let us not be ridiculous, my sister! I know what a fire is like. I have been in too many not to have complete respect for what is happening. Those fires are going to spread, and very fast. We must get to the Sumida River, at once."

The family packs their valuables into small sacks, places these on their shoulders, and under the constant prodding of Minetaro, leave the house for the distant river.

They are among the first people to take definite action. As they move out into the street, most of their neighbors are still wandering around in circles, staring at the fires in fear and awe. But none of them knows what to do.

Takeshi Nagamine, who was then twenty years old, and a student at Waseda University, recalls the moment: "We were not panicky, though, because Minetaro made our decision for us so quickly and with such firmness. My father, who died in 1949, was extraordinarily wary about fires, and knew their dangers well. He ordered us to go to the Sumida Park because the wind was blowing from the west. He realized that if the fires ever ran loose before the wind, the area was completely doomed—as were all the people who would be caught there. Around midnight, the wind was blowing at between twenty and thirty miles per hour. But after the fire bombs poured into the center of Honjo, the wind increased very quickly in strength. By the time we reached the park it was a full gale, blowing stronger than forty miles per hour.

"Although the fire presented a very grave danger, I was not frightened. We had just gone through the severe ordeal of having our home burned down around us in Minami Senju. And although hundreds of houses were burned and destroyed in the daylight attack, practically no one was killed. There was plenty of time to evacuate, and more than enough room to avoid the fires. So when we abandoned my aunt's home, it was without fear. We could not possibly imagine, except my father, what truly could happen."

The Nagamine family walks for about fifteen minutes, and then they reach the northern end of the Sumida Park, famed for its thousands of cherry trees. The branches are still bare; it is March, and too early for the brilliant blossoms.

The men, women, and children sit down in a corner of the park, Mrs. Nagamine looks around and speaks to her brother-in-law: "Minetaro, in the earthquake here so many years ago, I was away in an outer province when the shocks struck the city and the fires followed. But my parents and all my sisters and brothers were lost. They were seen along this river bank, some two miles to the south. There is reason to believe that they were not killed by the fires, but were pushed into the river by the hordes of people who panicked and fled the fires."

She looks around again nervously. "I do not think it wise that we remain here. I think we may request shelter at that mansion—over there." She points with her hand. "My friends live there and they will accommodate us. They have a very spacious garden and a deep pond."

Minetaro nods in assent: "You and Toshie must go there at once. However, my family are strangers to them, and we must not impose upon their hospitality. We shall remain here."

For the remainder of the long, flamed-filled night Mrs. Nagamine and her daughter Toshie cower in the garden, staying close by the pool and its water. They are fortunately away from the main spread of the flames, and for some unknown reason, away from the path that the terrorized mobs follow in their headlong dash from the fires. They watch the bombs falling in a terrible shower from the sky. The flames leap higher and higher as the two women remain hidden in the garden.

Over it all they suffer a constant, crashing din, a terrible staccato crackling and roaring and thunder. The noise

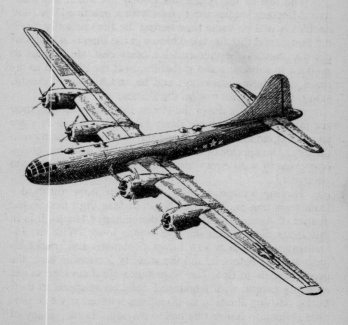

B-29 Superfortress

comes from the many sources, from the bombers and the anti-aircraft guns. The flames create a deep background, an unbelievable hissing, crackling roar, like a billion gas jets burning under full light. And there are other sounds, the cry of people, faint and weak, but swollen into a greater single sound because of the screaming from so many thousands of throats.

The wind is kind to them, and the firebrands and sparks that whirl like a blizzard before the wall of fire—a wall they see and look out upon with horror—blow away from their direction. Theirs is a night more of witnessing than of suffering, and they are grateful for the sharp insistence of Minetaro who has ordered them out of their own home.

The rest of the Nagamine family are much more active. Minetaro studies the flames with a practiced eye, and decides it will be some time before the fires actually reach the house, and that the wind blows in the direction that will not trap them if they return for a brief visit. He decides to go back to salvage some valuables, bids the children to remain with the maidservant, and he and his son, Takeshi, start out at a fast trot toward the flames.

As they move down the streets toward the house, they see more and more people fleeing in panic. The B-29's are an endless stream overhead, and the bombs are pouring into the city. The specter of the distant fires, the heat that grows oppressively with every minute, is enough to unnerve the strongest.

Having waited so long, the people now run madly from their homes. The fires begin to leap high first in the district of Asakusa, and next in the center of Honjo. It is in this latter district that the fire breaks loose. With the increasing wind which now blows firebrands and sparks almost straight before it, and the steadily increasing heat, the people decide to flee. The Nagamines are distressed to see so many people with frightened children strapped to their backs, dashing about in all directions without sense or purpose. Minetaro points this out to his son. "Look—many of them will burn tonight because they will end up running *into* the fire. Notice how few are running toward the park and the river where there will be safety."

Near the Kototoi Bridge, in Asakusa, a heavy battery of anti-aircraft guns erupts suddenly with savage explosions that crack with painful force against the ears. Minetaro and Takeshi stare in awe at the blasts of flame that spit from the gun muzzles; the heavy weapons are firing steadily, without respite, as fast as the gunners can pour shells into them.

It seems impossible that they can continue to fire, for the wind is driving a wall of flame, firebrands, and withering heat directly at them. Suddenly Minetaro grasps his son's arm and points upward. "Look—over there!" he shouts.

A great B-29 circles slowly, one wing trailing a long sheet of golden flame. The bomber slips and wallows helplessly, then falls in the distance toward Kawaguchi.

A shell explodes almost directly against the second B-29. Almost at once flame appears, this time in the body of the long silver giant. But it does not fall; the father and son watch it fly away, trailing fire.

TERROR AT THE BRIDGE

Kototoi is one of the eleven large steel bridges that spans the Sumida River in the city proper. It is the second bridge down from the northern limits of Tokyo. Like all the other steel bridges, Kototoi survived the war. But most of them were scenes of horrible carnage.

The bridge is about a hundred yards wide and just over two hundred yards long, a flat, paved surface that starts from Sumida Park, about three hundred yards south of where the Nagamine family took shelter from the flames.

The bridge is the center of a delayed-action but explosive evacuation by tens of thousands of people. The residents of Mukojima did not leave their homes early in the bombing; when the flames came closer, however, they flocked from their homes and assembled by the bridge. There they crowd together in a vast throng, accepting the Kototoi Bridge as a haven from the advancing fires. And for a while the bridge goes provide a refuge—but it is a false refuge, one that will disappear as the wind hurls the wall of fire closer and closer.

Across the river, in the Asakusa sector, the flames become a ravenous beast devouring everything in its path. Here there is terror beyond all belief. Most of the people in Asakusa make an error—a single error that is fatal. They remember the attack of February 25th against Minami Senju, which lies just to the north of Asakusa. The flames burned down many houses, but few people were killed or even injured.

So the citizens of the Asakusa area remain where they are even as the bombs rain from the sky. In the beginning there is time to flee, but that time vanishes with each new fire. Suddenly, before they realize what is happening, the entire Asakusa area is aflame.

There are some who remain, trying to fight the fires. The police and the civilian fire wardens, unaware that their battle is lost even before it starts, fight their courageous, hopeless struggle against the flames. They exhort the people to stand by their homes, to form bucket brigades, to transfer food and valuables into the small air-raid shelters beside their houses.

Thousands of people obey—and it is their sentence of death. They crowd into the shelters, jammed tightly, entire families together with other families. But in minutes the flames explode through the wood and paper houses. Cyclonic gusts of heat, white-hot, savage, explode and carom down the narrow alleys, flinging entire walls and ceilings before the furnace-like blasts.

A driving wind of sixty miles per hour and more hurls before it sparks and firebrands and burning timbers. Blazing doors and walls tumble along the streets. The small factories are filled with oil and grease and gasoline. The flames drive in, feed on the volatile mixtures, and the houses explode with the force of bombs, shattering the walls of nearby structures, hurling roaring balls of fire into the streets.

The shelters, into which thousands of people have jammed, are made of wood. Death comes with stark, gibbering agony, but the pain is short-lived. The tongues of flame, the balls of fire, the great crimson sheets, explode down the alleys and the streets, engulfing all before them.

Whole families in an instant were set aflame, roasting alive in unheard paroxysms of screaming and pain as the terrible heat exploded the wooden doors and supports of the shelters into flame. It is inevitable. The shelters are of wood. The wood is dry, surrounded by heat and fire.

The wind keeps the tidal wave low, pressing down the heat. It builds up to fantastic temperatures, past fifteen and eighteen hundred degrees. The shelters do not burn; they literally explode into flames, everything within explodes into flame.

The fire is like a river raging through a narrow channel. It rushes down an alley, writhes and boils in a dam of flame at the corners, and then spills out to follow its former course. It comes with terrifying suddenness, and the onslaught of that heat is simply too much to withstand.

In the shelter, a mother clasps her child; both in an instant are a blazing torch—hair, clothes, skin, everything in that split-second is afire. Shrieks tear from flaming throats, even as body liquids explode into steam. In the shelters the bodies do not even twist; they seem to writhe and vibrate; they quiver like a harpstring struck a savage blow. And then it is over.

There is a huge temple in Asakusa, the Kwannon Buddhist Temple. When the fires begin to streak through the slum section, tens of thousands of people remember the temple. Through the worst of the 1923 earthquake and fires the temple stood inviolate, untouched, a haven for all who flocked to its grounds. It was like a miracle.

Maddened by the flames, tens of thousands of people rush to the temple. Thousands jam into the huge structure. Outside the temple a living wall of humanity surges, people packed tightly against one another. Children with their mothers, the aged, all who can flee. Not all of them were able to reach the temple. Many hundreds have already been left behind.

The streets and the air are filled with sparks and firebrands. Most of the people are wearing clothes prime for fire. They have big fluffy coverings on their backs, or kimonos, or jackets. The instant that the clothes began to smoke or to show a spark the wearers tear them of. Now, their skin exposed to the heat, they begin to suffer. They pour toward the temple.

There are many who do not reach the haven they seek. Their clothes flame unexpectedly, or their hair burns, and they fall in the streets where the panic-stricken mob around them leaves them to die.

Once before, the Kwannon Buddhist Temple provided a miracle of safety. Tonight there is no miracle.

The sky fills with the swishing of the incendiaries as they pour down from the river of B-29's. Smoke boils along the ground, the firebrands mixed in. There is thunder and the roaring guns and the deep, sighing roar of the crowd. The holy structure is a goal to be reached at all costs, and the flames and noise only drive the people on to more frenzied efforts to reach safety inside.

Then a line of silvery bombers sails overhead at six thousand feet, and thousands of the magnesium fire bombs pour from the heavens. In minutes the great temple is blazing from end to end; the bombs have broken through the rooftop and crashed into the crowd. Magnesium charges explode in white-hot blinding flame.

Panic sweeps over the people jammed shoulder to shoulder within the temple. There is no room even to turn around! And it is into this jammed mass of humanity that the bombs fall. The magnesium tears into skin and hair and clothing. People recoil in agony and terror, they shriek with cries of the demented. There is a rush to get away, to flee.

In an instant the temple is absolute hell. There is no longer a crowd. The mass has become an insane beast, writhing to free itself of its own bonds. Children and women and men, young and old, are hurled to the floor of the temple. No one knows what happens, everything is blind, instinctive reaction.

Flee!

Get out!

The temple is aflame!

We will burn to death! *Burn!*

In seconds shoes crash into eyes and faces and ribs and noses and stomachs. Knees slam into groins and ribs. Bones snap like matchsticks as the beast of panic tears at itself, clawing and gouging. In those few seconds several hundred people are killed. People stand on the bodies, kick and punch and thrash in an attempt to claw their way free.

Near the great doors the mob pours outward like a river that has burst a dam. The stampede is absolutely unstoppable. The terror-stricken people crash in a wave against those still struggling to reach the temple. But behind the first wave of the fleeing mob there is more explosive panic. The heavy upper beams of the temple are burning fiercely and have begun to fall inward. Several break loose and come crashing down into the madly struggling crowd.

It is horrible beyond all description. In minutes thousands of men, women, and children meet death. Everything that takes place is animal. There are no descriptions from the survivors.

But the next day the police find *parts of bodies* strewn about like pieces of wood. The legs and arms of children, torn from their little bodies, lie in pools of dirt and dried blood. Fingers have been torn free. Many bodies are found with their chests caved completely in. Faces are unrecognizable. There are several thousand corpses lying on the ground—the majority untouched by flame.

The survivors erupt outward, shrieking and howling—into absolute, blazing hell.

For by now the tidal wave is upon them. The streets are white-hot with flame. Asakusa is like the belching orifice of a volcano. The streets are red hot, the asphalt bubbling, exploding everything that can possibly burn into wild, searing flames.

There are firemen out here in the streets, also attempting to escape. Their hose lines are burning, there is too little water pressure. The firemen tear free their couplings, clamber in fear aboard their trucks.

The mobs thunder outward from the temple—a temple that is now an enormous funeral pyre consuming the bodies still inside. The people rush upon the firetrucks, seeing in the vehicles a hope for salvation. Maddened by the terrible heat that cuts many down even as they run, driven insane by the flaming bodies still dashing along the streets, the mob pours over the firetrucks like a wave.

The humans turned to animal by fear claw and bite
and tear at the firemen, punch and gouge, drag them from
their seats. With strength born of fear they hurl the men
from the trucks as the savage fight progresses. The vehicles
wheel erratically under the hands of the maddened drivers.
They smash down people in the streets, crush the hapless
victims. Many of the trucks crash into buildings or weave
wildly into the flaming debris cascading down into the
streets.

The escape routes to the river no longer exist. The wall
of fire hangs in the sky, bears down upon the fleeing mobs.
The wind blows seemingly from all directions. The flame
pours in waves from buildings that a moment before stood
untouched. Fire lashes at both ends of the street, while in the
center hundreds of people cower in fear and horror. And then
the houses on each side explode violently into fire, and the
streets become a total sea of flames, engulfing and consuming
everything within reach.

It is impossible to plan the retreat. Blocks away untouched houses suddenly collapse under a horde of incendiaries, and explode into flame. Fire leaps up crazily on all
sides.

People are struck down as they stand or run. There is
no place to hide, no shelter, no safety. There is only fire.
Hundreds of people along the wide avenues of the firebreaks lie down in the center of the streets, huddling together. Flame does not come within hundreds of feet, but
suddenly the huddled forms explode into fire. Some leap
upward, run crazily for a few steps, then collapse, twisting
like crumpled flower stalks, until they lie still, smoldering.
Many others simply do not move. They burn. They die.

Thousands succeed in forcing their way to the west
bank of the river. Here there is a park, but it is very narrow,
no more than a hundred yards in its width. Made to hold
just a few hundred people, it soon overflows with thousands. Behind the park there are only flames, blazing
houses, intolerable heat.

The wind blows toward the river, and the flotsam of
the mass fires descends in a grisly shower upon the crowd.
The firebrands set them aflame, and there is too little room

even to tear off clothes. It is impossibly, suffocatingly hot, and people drop like flies.

The children especially gasp for breath—they suck in the superheated air. Spasms wrack their bodies, there is a final convulsive jerk, and then stillness. Others leap into the river; with nothing to grasp, they cannot stay afloat, and by the hundreds they drown.

Those on the banks are no more fortunate. For the flames bear down with terrible speed.

Not one human soul survives.

15

CITY OF TERROR

Several thousand people who survived the crush from the Buddhist temple break free of the seething mobs. They are apprehensive that if they remain along the river banks, the flames will reach out to them. Moving as a herd of cattle following a single leading animal, the throng stampedes with hoarse shouts and cries to the Kototoi Bridge.

But the bridge is already filled. It is black with human beings who have poured onto its surface from the other side of the river.

The two panic-stricken mobs meet and clash in a savage, ruthless struggle in the center of the bridge.

The surge of the desperate, burned mob from Asakusa is too great to stop. They pour as a solid wedge into the other refugees. The thousands of adults and children shriek in a cataclysm of horror, but the sound is scarcely heard above the gunblasts of the anti-aircraft battery alongside the bridge.

The two throngs clash into one another, and the Asakusa mob continues to push ahead in a solid mass of bodies. At the edges of the bridge people are crushed against the railings. Others are pushed off the bridge and into the water, more than one hundred and fifty feet below. Very few survive.

By now the wall of fire, the advancing tidal wave, is much closer. It flings ahead of it a spray of burning wood, firebrands, sparks, large chunks of blazing timber. This constant shower pours into the maddened people driving them to even greater frenzy.

But what is worse is the rain of the magnesium fire bombs; many of these fall directly into the mass of people on the bridge. When a bomb strikes a person, it is an instant death sentence. But incendiary material showers outward, it sizzles and sputters and burns with its skin-destroying touch. Each such bomb is the center of another bed of horror as the mad strike blindly out in order to escape.

There is yet another rain from the skies. Tokyo is thick with anti-aircraft guns, and tens of thousands of shells pour into the heavens. After they burst, the shrapnel falls back into the city in a lethal hail. It is impossible to estimate how many hundreds who were exposed and in the open died from the effects of the falling, jagged metal debris. The next day the police are able to identify several dozen corpses, victims of shrapnel; the others will never be known, for the bodies are either completely consumed or are totally unrecognizable.

In minutes the river is the only hope for escape. By the hundreds, the people climb the railings and leap into the water. Most are stunned by their impact with the river from a fall of one hundred and fifty feet. Others die quickly from shock, for it is March and the water is bitter cold. Even the most expert swimmers find it exceedingly difficult just to stay alive. Very few of those who take to the water survive.

Not one human being on the bridge remains alive. When the mass finally ceases to writhe, it begins to smolder from the constant flood of firebrands and sparks. The heat radiates outward from the nearby shores. Tongues of fire lick upward. But only the external surfaces of the tightly-packed bodies burn. The rest of the mass smolders and smokes. The stench is nauseating. When the rescue operations begin here the next day, many of the bodies are melted together and cannot be pried apart.

THE OVENS OF TOKYO

The Honjo ward, miles away, becomes at the same time another scene of hideous, flaming carnage.

The young housewife we encountered earlier, Mrs. Mizuta, like many others, has underestimated the magnitude of the great fires. When she leaves her home with her five-year-old son and her aged parents, the air is already blistering hot. The skies are filled with pieces of burning debris. The streets are filled with people dashing madly, in pain and panic.

Over the increasing din, Mrs. Mizuta shouts to her parents: "Stay close to my side! We must hold our hands together—let us to go the Futaba School!"

The three adults and the youngster walk no further than a block when suddenly a swarm of incendiary bombs crashes across the width of the street right before them. Instantly the flaming mass splatters in every direction. Flames erupt from the buildings on both sides of the street.

They turn, quickly, seeking a detour. But now the very sky around and above them becomes a howling blizzard of fire particles. Houses explode into flames in the front, the back, to their sides, cascading blazing wreckage into the streets, sending out heat so intense that it blisters their skin.

Everywhere they turn there is fire. The wind roars wildly through the streets. People run with arms before their faces as a shield, moaning piteously as their clothes suddenly turn into sheets of fire. Dozens of people, young and old, burn alive. Children dash to and fro, shrieking in tortured, shrill voices, hurling themselves down on sidewalks, or running wildly into the fire. The streets are thick with smoking corpses.

Their hearts sick with fear, the Mizuta family cowers, and at the bidding of the mother wisely drop to the ground. They begin to crawl toward the end of the street. Flaming pieces of wood constantly strike their bodies. The two old people protect each other and help the mother, who is busy slapping at the firebrands that fall onto the body of her ashen-faced, shocked son.

Mrs. Mizuta never knows when the knapsack she is carrying disappears, or what became of the blanket she is carrying for her boy. They are just gone.

The world is a terrifying nightmare. Mrs. Mizuta worries only for the safety of her child, and she shields his body with her own as the firebrands land on her back, her legs and neck and head. Finally she reaches the school.

Her elderly parents are gone—vanished. Somewhere, something has happened to them. But it is impossible to turn back. Behind her there is a living wall of fire.

People mill about helplessly at the school entrance. Holding her son close to her side, Mrs. Mizuta attempts to force her way into the building. It is a hopeless task, the thousands of people around the building form a solid, immovable wall of humanity.

Several times more she tries, running to each entrance of the school, but she cannot get in.

Now the child, terrified and silent since he left home, speaks up for the first time. "Mommy, it's hot. I'm so hot. Let's go home, Mommy."

The plaintive wail of her child snaps Mrs. Mizuta back to reality. She realizes for the first time how cruelly hot the air has become, and her folly in attempting to force her way into a building that is already packed with refugees. Even if they were to escape the flames, the first signs of panic would doom her and the child to a death either by being trampled underfoot, or by suffocation.

She grasps the boy tightly by his hand, and walks away rapidly, toward the Sumida River. The decision saves their lives.

They cross two blocks, Mrs. Mizuta shielding the boy from the intense heat and the fury of the swirling, firebrand-filled air. Then they dash across a wide avenue, and reach a small shrine that stands as a dedication to 32,000 victims of the 1923 earthquake and fire who died in this area. A sparse crowd already fills the small compound, and more are pouring in with every minute. There is room for the mother and child, but Mrs. Mizuta does not like the shrine, and its association with a terrible past tragedy.

They keep moving. Behind the shrine is a small public park, with elaborate gardens and ponds, owned formerly by a wealthy baron. But the grounds are crowded with refugees from the flames. Again there is room; again, however, Mrs. Mizuta is wise. She notices that on both sides of the park there are rows of houses. She is fully aware now of the power of the flames advancing behind her. They go on.

After another ten minutes of flight they arrive at the spacious plaza that stretches before the Ryogoku Railroad Station. Behind the station is a sprawling marshalling yard; it is almost empty of cars. Mrs. Mizuta looks around. There are no houses nearby, only buildings of concrete and steel.

They will remain here. Gratefully, Mrs. Mizuta sinks to the ground, wrapping her child in her clothing. Soon the plaza begins to fill with people. They all drop to the ground, sitting or squatting. All of the people here survive the flames.

Not until the following day does Mrs. Mizuta learn that of the three thousand men, women, and children jammed into the Futaba School, only *fifteen* survived.

There is the story of Hidezo Tsuchikura, a factory worker, who, with his two young children, spent the night at the Futaba School and emerged alive.

"By some miracle I survived the worst of the 1923 disaster. I was only six years of age then, and all I remembered at the time was the sudden shock and the earth heaving; the next thing I knew the house had collapsed on top of me. Rescuers dug me out, still unconscious, from beneath a great mound of charred bodies where the memorial shrine now stands.

"Everything happened too fast, and I was too young to be really frightened by what happened then. But I never forgot the details, or the aftermath. So when the bombers started to pour fire into Tokyo in the mass incendiary raid, I had absolutely no intention of remaining outside in an open space. I wanted something overhead to protect my two children and myself. The moment the bombs started to fall, we all ran to the school building. Fortunately, my wife and our newborn child were away in an outlying province.

"We were among the first arrivals in the school compound. The children seemed to regard the whole affair as something gay; they had no real reason yet to be frightened. The school stood three stories high, and was of rectangular shape. On the eastern side there was a large swimming pool separated from a twenty-yard alley by a six-foot-high concrete wall. The southern part of the building on the ground floor was a large indoor gym. The outdoor playground was not large but it was protected by other concrete buildings of three stories in height. There was also a large basement section, expanded as an air-raid shelter, that could hold at least five hundred persons.

"I went to the basement first. But several minutes later I was convinced that this was no place of safety; refugees poured in steadily. If there was ever a panic, or the building collapsed, there would be no hope for my children to be dug out from under the mass of people—as I was in 1923.

"We went outside again; I looked around and decided that the gym would be safest. It had wide doors and was near the swimming pool. But within another ten minutes, coming in through three doors, more than a thousand persons crowded into the gym.

"Many of them carried some personal effects and valuables with them. Each person carried only a little, but when a thousand people are added up, it becomes quite something. I became uneasy as my eyes grew accustomed to the darkness. Again I changed my mind and pushed my way out. I took the children upstairs to the second floor, and we sat down behind the door. But again, in no time at all, the room filled with a solid mass of people. By this time, I could see from the windows that the fires were advancing rapidly toward the school.

"I just couldn't stay in a place that was so crowded. We again left, and walked up to the third floor and into another classroom.

"The fires were incredible by now, with flames leaping hundreds of feet into the air. There seemed to be a solid wall of fire rolling toward the building. All the windows were closed to prevent sparks from pouring into the rooms and setting the school ablaze.

"Still the people poured in! The halls were now jammed and every last room was filled. With so many people inside the air was rapidly becoming stifling. It had an ominous, sultry feeling about it. I was uneasy and not a little frightened. Many people were already gasping for breath. With every passing minute the air became more and more foul.

"But the people were so frightened that they refused to open the windows. My children were weakening visibly. They begged me to take them home. Every child seems to believe that his home is always comfortable and safe, no matter what is happening.

"I did not want to leave, but the sight of the children's suffering decided my course of action. This time I made the drastic decision to go out to the roof. It meant breaking a lifelong obsession against staying out in the open. Without the children, however, I would never have made the move.

"Again we climbed the staircase, stepping over and around the people lying on the stairs. More than one person reproached me for going out to the roof, but I didn't care what anyone had to say.

"On the roof it was like stepping into hell. Pieces of flaming wood and sparks rained down from the sky or shot horizontally through the air. The night was terribly hot, but even this was a tremendous relief over what we had been forced to breathe. I watched the children inhaling deeply and smiling for the first time in many minutes. It was worth it. We sat down near a water tank.

"I told the children to stay down and stood up to see what was happening. The rooftop was lit up much brighter than if it were broad daylight. Flames leaped high over the city, and the noise was a continuing, crashing roar. The great bombers were still coming over Tokyo in an endless stream.

"I looked over the edge of the roof, looking down, and my heart stopped. I could not believe what I saw. It was a scene out of the worst possible nightmare, and in all the years since that night I have been unable to forget a single detail.

"Fire-winds filled with burning particles rushed up and down the streets. I watched people—adults and children—running for their lives, dashing madly about like rats. The flames raced after them like living things, striking them down. They died by the hundreds right in front of me. Wherever I turned my eyes, I saw people running away from the school grounds seeking air to breathe. They raced away from the school into a devil's cauldron of twisting, seething fire. The whole spectacle with its blinding lights and thundering noise reminded me of the paintings of Purgatory. Yes, that was it—a real Inferno straight out of the depths of hell itself!

"I was stunned and appalled and spellbound, and waves of dizziness swept over me. I became faint, and the world began to spin.

"The children saved my life. My five-year-old daughter, Masayo, was screaming at me. Her cries aroused me from the stupor into which I had fallen. When I opened my eyes and looked up I almost screamed in horror.

"Sparks had landed on her back, and her clothes were starting to blaze. I scooped water from the nearby tank and frantically beat my hands against the flames. By a miracle I put out the fire before it could spread and harm the child. And in that same instant my boy, Shoji, screamed that he too was on fire.

"Desperately I grasped my son, lifted him bodily, and plunged him into the water tank. It saved his life.

"There was no respite. Masayo pointed at me and shrieked that *I* was burning. I dropped the boy, soaking wet, and leaped into the tank to douse the flames.

"For the next ninety minutes or so we kept repeating this procedure. The air was so hot that as I doused the children and put them back on the roof the water steamed almost immediately from their clothes.

"We were extraordinarily fortunate. By three o'clock in the morning the fire had reached the last houses that lay in its path. The great flames began to die out. We huddled together for another two hours, my back to the water tank, the children buried in my arms.

"Then about five o'clock I saw the first signs of dawn. I took Masayo and Shoji by the hands, and started for the staircase. It was only ten yards from where we had spent the entire night. When I arrived at the door I could not believe my eyes.

"More than a dozen people were sprawled about in grotesque positions. Every one of them was dead. The wooden parts of the staircase glowed red, smoldering with live embers. Smoke filled the hallway and the stench nearly made me vomit. It was impossible to go on down. I told the children to remain where they were and looked further down the stairway. It was horrible. Hundreds of bodies were lying on the stairs and the floors, smoking and steaming.

"We turned to the other two stairways, but we encountered the same situation. By this time we had discovered that another twelve persons had dared to weather the night on the rooftop. We were the only survivors of the entire building.

"We clustered together in a group, but everyone was so stunned by the catastrophe that we did little talking. We did agree, however, that we must wait several more hours until everything within the school building could burn itself out before we could try to get away.

"Then, an hour later, one of the men discovered an emergency fire stairway made of iron. He led the rest of us down by walking in front and flinging away the burning and smoldering objects that had fallen on the iron stairs.

"What had happened confirmed my worst fears. The entire building had become a huge oven three stories high. Every human being inside the school was literally baked or boiled alive in heat. Dead bodies were everywhere in grisly heaps. None of them appeared to be badly charred. They looked like mannequins, some of them with a pinkish complexion.

"Strangely enough, there were only a few bodies in the playground. Evidently the asphalt surface had burst into flame, turning the playground into a wide pool of fire, and preventing escape along this route.

"But the swimming pool was the most horrible sight of all. It was hideous. More than a thousand people, we estimated, had jammed into the pool. The pool had been filled to its brim when we first arrived. Now there wasn't a drop of water, only the bodies of the adults and children who had died.

"We gave thanks for our safety and hurried away. I had seen things that I will not forget for the rest of my life."

Senko Hayashi, who had sent her parents on to the Futaba School—never to see them again—never reached the school building herself. As she emerges from her home and runs as quickly as she can toward the Futaba School, she stops short in horror, staring with shocked eyes at the monstrous cyclone of fire that screams high into the air, lashes downward, and leaps across a fifty-yard-wide fire lane along the street of Isiwara.

Senko spins on her heel, and runs into an alley that will take her to the school along a different route. Again she is stopped in her tracks as a twisting mass of flame boils toward her from the far end of the alley. She screams in terror and runs back to the main street. Flames are all around her, and her lungs are burning as she sucks in the superheated air. She beats constantly at her clothing, feels her lips and eyes scorching from the terrible heat.

There is only one chance, and Senko Hayashi does not hesitate. On her hands and knees in the middle of the street, braving the worst of the fiery gusts, she begins to crawl toward a wider fire lane that runs from Ryogoku to the east, along a line perhaps a half-mile south of Futaba. This is her story:

"I cannot to this day remember how I managed to force my way through the flames and the heat to reach the firebreak beneath the overhead railway. When I arrived at this haven in the midst of the burning city, I was startled to see that I had lost everything I was carrying. Everything I had taken from the house—the knapsack, the blanket, even my cap—was gone.

"Had I been forced to drag along a small child, like Mrs. Mizuta, or had I carried a baby on my back, I know I would never have survived. I would simply have collapsed on the road and died there, just as did so many mothers with their infants in their arms.

"I cowered in the midst of the firebreak for hours that I cannot recall. There were thousands of people around me, and not until daybreak did the great roaring flames begin to subside. When it was clear that the fires were dying down, we looked at each other in disbelief. We were alive! It was true, we were really alive!

"I struggled to my feet and began to walk toward the

Futaba School, convinced I would find my parents there, safe and sound. By the time I arrived at the school, I was completely numb with horror, and afraid to admit that I might never find my parents alive. Soldiers were already at the school, dragging out the thousands of bodies and lining them up on the streets and in the playground. Other soldiers were in the swimming pool, carrying out the bodies.

"I bit my lip and went in. My brain was numb, I was in a state of shock as I walked up and down the lines of bodies, trying to identify my mother and father. Then I went to the poolside and watched the bodies, already bloated, being laid out on the ground. Again I failed to recognize my parents.

"There were many other people in similar straits, searching for their loved ones. I was amazed at my calmness. I was not weeping or hysterical. I was completely emotionless, almost detached from my own body. I had seen so many horrible things that even these corpses could not make an impression upon me. I remember walking around in a daze for many hours, searching hopelessly for my parents. Then I walked back to the ruins of my home."

The members of the Tsukakoshi family were among the tens of thousands who fled to the Futaba area:

"I was the last to abandon home," Hisashi Tsukakoshi said quietly. "After reaching the street, I was stunned to realize how long I must have taken. The whole city seemed to be on fire. I was nearly overwhelmed with the heat, the screaming noise, the burning, shocking flames.

"I knew that I had delayed so long that I could never reach the Futaba School. Instead I turned and ran toward the firebreak where there would be safety. I was then a young man of twenty-seven, but even so I found it extraordinarily difficult to fight my way through the blazing streets.

"I had to run into the winds. Time and time again terrific blasts of heat and wind smashed me from my feet. Each time I got up and staggered until I was hurled to the ground again. There were very few people able to move. I saw many bodies on the ground, burning fiercely.

"Burning debris showered all over me, the embers and sparks sticking mercilessly to my clothing. Several times my clothes flared up in a blaze, and I had to stop to beat out the fires.

"By the time I was only one block from the firebreak, I felt that I was about to collapse. I simply couldn't go on. I gasped for air and tried to suck in air to breathe, but all that I brought in was a mass of scorching air that was agony in my throat and lungs. I felt I would die right where I was.

"I was choking to death, and I could do nothing about it. I clung helplessly to a telephone pole, fighting to prevent my collapse to the pavement. If I fell, I knew that I was finished.

"The street was about fifty yards wide. On both sides of me were houses blazing fiercely. Many of them came crashing down with the roar of an avalanche. Cyclones of fire whirled about everywhere I looked, and I could feel my skin starting to blister. Strangely, I felt no pain. If I was to die, I thought, at least it will be quietly and without any thrashing about.

"I cannot remember how long I clung to the pole, unable to move.

"Then I noticed an elderly man dash out of a house that erupted in flames as he came rushing from the doorway. He ran toward me. Five feet away he stumbled, tried to cry out, but collapsed to the pavement. He tried to rise, but could not. He placed both hands on the ground, trying to force himself up, but it was more than he could do.

"I stared at him, my mouth gaping. His legs moved and his shoulders heaved, but he simply could not lift his head. He looked like a man who had been frozen while trying to get up after stretching out in a prayer ceremony on the floor.

"A firebrand whirled out of the sky and crashed onto his cap. Instantly this burst into flames. It was the sight that forced me to move my frozen limbs. I remember thinking through a blur that I could not let this old man burn alive right in front of me. I had to help him.

"Somehow I staggered to his side. I bent down, trying to beat out the flames on his cap. It was impossible, and with every passing second the fire spread. Soon tufts of hair on his neck were burning.

"I pulled at the cap in an attempt to remove it from his head. But it was tied tightly by a string beneath the man's neck. I could not break the strings or undo the knot. I strained with all my might, but by now I was weak and sickly.

"Suddenly with a wave of horror I discovered that my own clothes were blazing! I ripped my own cap from my head and flung it away. I beat on my jacket and trousers to put out the flames. Immediately I felt completely exhausted all over again. I staggered back to the telephone pole and leaned against it weakly.

"I turned to look at the elderly man on the street. His cap was burning, but the body did not move. He was dead; killed by the heat.

"I forced myself out of the daze and began to struggle toward the firebreak. Houses burned on each side of me and again and again I beat out flames with my bare hands—but I felt nothing except an overwhelming weariness. I gasped and choked for air, and somehow I managed to reach the wide safety lane beneath the elevated railway. There was no room to lie down. I squatted numbly, and just closed my eyes. Breathing was still difficult, but it was infinitely better here than in the midst of the flames."

Shortly after four in the morning the towering flames subsided quickly; there was nothing left in their path to burn. The people who had waited out the fires rose to their feet, with hardly a word spoken, and began to drift away. Hisashi Tsukakoshi was one of the thousands.

He stared numbly at the city he knew so well. The blocks were burned right to the ground. He walked through a smoldering, ash-choked wilderness. By some miracle he was hardly burned at all; he could not believe his good fortune for a while, but soon came to realize that the hand of fate had rested upon his shoulders.

Soon, however, his eyes began to hurt. Within thirty minutes both eyes felt like they were blazing coals; the pain was intense and constant. Everyone on the streets suffered the same agony, a result of serious overexposure to smoke.

Hisashi walked on and on, rubbing his wounded eyes. Tears poured down his cheeks. But as with so many of the other survivors the tears were involuntary, a result of eye injury. He was numbed beyond any emotion other than his desire to find his family. Knowing how close to death he had come, he did not feel they would be alive.

Presently he passed the street corner where he had stopped and waited for death to come. The old man was still lying in the street, like a statue toppled over. The clothes were burned from his body, yet the flesh itself was not charred. Neither was there any sign of agony on his face. Hisashi Tsukakoshi stared in shocked, numb wonder, and wandered away.

At the next street corner, the sight before him reached down through his shock and jarred his very soul. A mother and her child, about three years old, were dead. The woman was on her knees, erect, the baby strapped to her back. All their clothes had been burned away, but again the bodies were scarcely touched.

The woman's head was turned, her hands reaching out to hold her child, to bring the daughter to her arms. They had both died in this position, a silent prayer by the mother for her child.

Hisashi turned his head away, and stumbled down the street, walking around the corpses that littered the ground.

He saw two hands sticking out from an oil drum. He looked in. The water that had been kept in the drum was gone. There was a body inside—the body of a man who had climbed into the drum of water and then had suffocated from the heat.

He reached his home—the smoking ashes of what had been his home. The entire area was leveled to the ground. For more than four hours Hisashi Tsukakoshi sat numbly on the ground, not knowing what to do, where to go, drowning in his grief.

A hand tapped on his shoulder. Hisashi looked up, startled. It was a friend. "I am glad to see you," the man said quietly. "You are fortunate, my friend. I have just seen Yoshiko and your child. They are safe—they are now at the Midori School where they are resting."

Hisashi leaped to his feet, stammered his words of gratitude, and found hidden strength to run. The Midori Primary School was several blocks south of the railway firebreak. It was a smaller school than the building at Futaba, but by a miracle it had survived the flames. Ironically, few people sought shelter there, preferring to go to Futaba in the belief that the swimming pool meant safety.

Minutes later, he rejoined his wife. Tears of joy streamed down the cheeks of the couple. Hisashi learned that Yoshiko had arrived at the firebreak after turning away from the Futaba School. She had spent the entire night only fifty yards from where he had sat!

Two hours later, the overjoyed couple found their parents. They were one of the very few families in the thick of the flames to survive intact.

Seaman Recruit Yasuichi Mizuta, then twenty-seven years old, was granted a one-week pass by the Yokosuka Naval Station when his commanding officer learned that his home was in downtown Tokyo. On March 12th, he returned to the ruins of his home, not knowing whether he would find his wife and child alive.

"From the Ryogoku station," he recalls, "I could see across the miles of ruins. I saw trains that were four miles away—and nothing stood between me and the trains. The entire area had been flattened, was ashes.

"I cried with joy when in the midst of all this devastation I found my wife at the ruins of our home. We embraced; I learned that our boy Makato was also safe. But my parents were gone forever.

"For the next week I stayed with Kikue and our son at the Midori School, living and sleeping in the gym. I spent my days searching for my parents. Occasionally, in the midst of the ruins, I encountered old friends. They told me of their horrible experiences; it was an indirect means of informing me also that my aged mother and father could not possibly have survived the holocaust.

"One man told me he was the only survivor of his family—six had died. They had gone to the Kikugawa Creek, about a mile east of my home. The creek was only twenty yards wide, running from Mukojima to Tokyo Bay.

Every foot of the creek was choked with bodies—the official estimates said more than ten thousand people had died in the waterway.

"My friend and his family went into the water, and lined up along the bank. Houses on both sides of them burned fiercely. Then one by one his family began to choke and to faint. They slipped away before his horrified gaze.

"He tried to go to their help, to save his children. But each time he moved he was seized with a spasm of coughing that brought blood up from his lungs, and he slipped beneath the water. He fought his way up again, half dead. When he could see, he cried out in anguish. Within fifteen minutes he was the only person left.

"The heat beat down upon him like unending physical blows. His lungs were tortured and his throat raw. All his strength was gone. He locked his fingers on the bank and just lay there, too weak to move.

"When I met him, he was living a thousand deaths. To see your own family die right before you when you are helpless to do anything about it!

"The stench in the area, the cremation of the bodies by the police and health officials, the hovering smell of the incendiary bombs made people sick, over and over again. After several days of fruitless searching for my parents, I sent my wife and child off to some relatives who lived on a farm, many miles from Tokyo.

"There, at least, they would be safe."

The Nagamine family at Mukojima greeted the close of the fire attack and the first signs of daylight with "an inexpressible feeling of vast relief." They are just grateful that they are alive; there are no feelings of hate directed toward the enemy, no bitterness at the failure of their leaders to stop the attack, nor even sorrow at the losses around them. Emotions have fallen into a bottomless pit; they know only relief and gratitude.

Minetaro Nagamine, the father, decides to take his two daughters—Hideko, 17, and Katsuyo, 15—as well as his niece, Toshie, 15, and their maidservant, to his brother's home in Saitama, on a farm fifty miles to the north of Tokyo.

Mrs. Nagamine chooses to remain in Tokyo, for one of the houses the family owns in Mukojima has survived the devastation. The irony of the blaze in this areas is that scores of Geisha houses and many swank restaurants remained virtually untouched by the flames, while almost every house and every factory burned to the ground.

Takeshi Nagamine, the student, also decides to stay in order to resume his work at Waseda University.

"Shortly after daybreak," Takeshi relates, "I went to visit a friend in Asakusa—or really to see if my friend and his family had survived the fires. I left about nine in the morning, and had I known the terrible slaughter that had taken place, I would never have started. Having remained in the park all night, we knew only of the great flames and that there was some fire damage, but that was all."

Takeshi reached the Kototoi Bridge several minutes later. The sight before him was overwhelming; he held his breath in horror as he saw the thousands of bodies on, beneath, and on both sides of the bridge. He threaded his way through the mass of corpses, many of them piled six and seven deep. Soldiers were already on the scene, arranging the bodies in even rows for identification.

"All the bodies were naked, but not charred," Takeshi said. "The skin color was only slightly more pink-brown than was normal, just like those of store-window mannequins. But their clothes, belongings and hair were completely burned. Many of their faces bore expressions of agony and terror. There were more than six thousand bodies around the bridge. . . ."

Thousands of corpses floated on the surface of the river, and soldiers were hooking bodies drifting beneath the surface. The dead Japanese were everywhere—in the park, on the river banks, in the water, on the roads.

Indeed, six months later, after the war was over, Japanese police were still searching the waters beneath the Kototoi Bridge for the victims of the March 10th fires. Those that were recovered from the river bottom were buried at once in the west bank park area, which was turned into a graveyard to hold the hundreds of bodies unexpectedly discovered months later.

Takeshi crossed the Kototoi Bridge and soon reached the wide avenue that cuts through Asakusa, and then continued on down to the Ginza, Tokyo's Broadway, some four miles to the south. He passed a six-story department store on the other side of the bridge, and again the area was littered with hundreds of bodies.

"Here the bodies were charred beyond recognition," he recalls, "indicating that the fire was intense and close. During the night, I saw the flames leaping high through the buildings in the sector.

"All the bodies I saw were black. Near the pavement I found what seemed to be two children hugging each other in their death. I went closer. They were not children, but adults, judging from the man's full-size steel helmet and other metal debris lying around. Evidently I was seeing the remains of a husband and wife, but they were terribly shrunken in size. The charred and shrunken heads looked like those of dolls. It was an incredible thing to see—even after watching the thousands of bodies on the bridge. My stomach felt as though it would never stop its churning."

Takeshi Nagamine turned to the right and walked toward his friend's home. The streets he passed along were strewn with lesser numbers of the dead. When he arrived at his friends' house he found only ashes. The entire area for block after block was completely gutted and leveled.

In dismay he went to the nearby Sensoku Primary School that he knew was used as a shelter. As he approached the buildings his hopes soared; the building stood intact. But when he stepped inside he recoiled as if from a physical blow. The interior was burned to cinders, including mounds that could only be bodies.

He went down to the basement shelter. Again he saw only bodies, more than four hundred corpses heaped and piled in grotesque positions. In despair Takeshi tried to identify the body of his friend.

"All the bodies in the basement appeared at first sight to be exactly like the mummies I had seen in museums," he said. "The entire basement had become an oven. Every person seemed to have been baked under an extraordinarily high fire. The corpses were dried up, shriveled, and black. They were completely naked. Their clothes and everything else in the basement that could burn was gone. I made several efforts to look at the faces of the bodies, but then I could stand no more. I ran up the stairs and outside, where I retched."

He sat weakly on the curb. He could see for miles across the Asakusa area. He saw the Ueno Hill, two miles to the west, and another five miles to the east across the river. He was astonished to note that the huge Buddhist temple had burned to the ground.

He trudged wearily back home, and rejoined his aunt. That afternoon he borrowed a bicycle to travel to Honjo in the hope of finding another friend in that area.

He found only death and leveled areas. Corpses littered the streets. His friend's home was gone. He pedaled on for miles. The Wholesaler's Town in Nihonbashi was a desert of ashes. The famed Meiji-za Theater had become a slaughterhouse. Packed with more than a thousand people, it had suddenly exploded into flames and trapped everyone inside, roasting its victims.

Numb with shock at what he had witnessed, he turned to the mound of ashes that had been his home.

AFTERMATH

When the sun rose on Tokyo on the morning of March 10th, the terrible winds had died away. The day was clear and cold. Most of the great fires had died down, burning themselves out among the big concrete buildings. The rivers marked the edge of the astounding, terrible areas of destruction. The heart of Tokyo, its most densely populated area, was a garish wasteland of ash.

Here and there, poking upward from the desert, a lone building still blazed, the orange flames licking up from the wasteland. The bodies were everywhere, blackened and charred. Telephone poles stood garishly against the bleak and empty skyline, their tips still burning, glowing red-hot and giving off wisps of white smoke.

There were buildings still standing—the concrete schools, the steel factories. There were thousands of chimneys, naked and obscene. But that was all. And almost every one of the buildings was gutted inside.

Tokyo had become a monstrous, diseased flatness. The people moved slowly or squatted on the ground. They were numb, drained of emotion, distantly grateful that the fires were gone and they were alive. Their eyes teared from the smoke, their throats were raw, and many had severe blisters and burns.

The Army moved in and set up aid stations and food centers. The survivors in the gutted area lined up silently, shuffling along like mummies. They did not talk, they had no desire to talk.

There was very little noise in Tokyo. Every now and

then a brick wall, standing alone, would collapse, and there would be a light rumble of bricks. No one turned to look.

The police were busy. They took charge of the dead, collecting the corpses in great piles, pouring gasoline on the bodies, and then burning them. A blue-white smoke drifted across the city, heavy and sweetish and gut-wrenching with its smell of death.

The fire chief of Tokyo informed the Emperor that he considered the city absolutely helpless against my further attacks. The entire telephone alarm system was destroyed; it would be impossible to rebuild it for at least six months or more.

Thousands of bodies were recovered that had been *boiled*. It took time for this to sink in, but it was the literal truth. People in the shallower canals, where they had gone for safety, died horribly when the water in the canal boiled, and cooked the occupants to death.

"People running for refuge were trapped by the bombings ahead and around them," states an official report of the attack, "and were encircled with flames and black smoke. They looked for protection to the canals and rivers, but in some districts the shallow canals were boiling from the heat which seemed to be compressed by the wind, and the canals were full of people. In some places one swarm of humanity after another crowded into the water and by the time a third or fourth wave of frantic people had jumped, the first wave lay on the bottom. Those who survived the ordeal were burned around the head and neck by the constant rain of sparks.

"Fire-fighting equipment proved pitifully inadequate. The firemen rushed to a burning area and worked until the fire there got beyond their control, then they went elsewhere. They tried to concentrate their efforts on the big factories, but the results were almost unnoticeable. Ninety-six fire engines, 150 hand-drawn gasoline-driven pumps, and 65,000 feet of hose were burned. Eighty-five firemen were dead from the fire, 40 missing, and the casualties of the auxiliary police and the fire units came to more than 600. Forty per cent of the capital city was burned to the ground."

By official estimate, more than 130,000 people were dead.

Sixteen square miles of Tokyo were gone.

But it was only the beginning of a hurricane of fire that would soon sweep up and down the Japanese islands.

Two days after the attack, 286 of the great B-29 raiders were over the city of Nagoya, attacking a three-mile-long triangular area in Japan's third largest industrial center. The crews reported that the city looked "like a gigantic bowling center with all the alleys lighted up; each flight had left an alley of flames." But Nagoya was more modern than Tokyo, filled with fire-resistant modern structures, and defended by the best fire department in Japan. Only 1.56 miles were burned out, but these included vital industrial targets, Nagoya went on the list for unfinished business.

Osaka was next—the third largest port in Japan and a center of heavy industry. On the night of March 14th, 2,240 tons of fire bombs ripped the heart of the city into a flaming holocaust. By morning the city had lost nearly nine square miles—and its greatest factories—totally destroyed.

Three days later a total of 2,300 tons of bombs poured into Kobe, sixth largest city of Japan, and a major rail and highway transportation center. Three square miles of Japan's largest concentration of shipbuilding and marine-engine plants vanished in flames.

"Fifth and last attack in the series," reported an A.A.F. editor, "was made on the return trip to Nagoya when again more than 300 B-29's dropped some 2,000 tons on the city. Overcompensating for the scattered bombing on the previous attack, the bombs were dropped in too small an area, and only .65 square miles of the city were destroyed. But nobody doubted, least of all the Japanese, that the blitz was a holocaust. In five missions more than 29 square miles of Japan's chief industrial centers were burned out beneath a rain of bombs that totaled 10,100 tons. By comparison, on the Luftwaffe's greatest fire raid on London, only 200 tons were dropped. And on the Eighth Air Force's record strike on Berlin (3 February 1945), over 1,000 heavy bombers made a 1,000-mile round trip to drop 2,250 tons. During the ten-day blitz, nearly this same tonnage was carried *on each mission* by only 300 B-29's. The round trip exceeded 3,200 miles.

"Our losses to AA and fighters were less than 1.3 per cent of aircraft over the target, and they were soon to drop even lower. Greatest source of alarm to our flyers were the terrific thermals, or hot-air currents, that rose from the blazing targets and sent out aircraft into a black hell of smoke. One B-29 commander related what happened over Osaka:

" 'We headed into a great mushroom of boiling, oily smoke, and in a few seconds were tossed 5,000 feet into the air. It was a jerky, snappy movement. The shock was so violent that I felt I was losing consciousness. "This is it," I thought, "I can't pull out of it." Smoke poured into the ship and every light was blacked out. It smelled like singed hair, or a burning damp heap. Everybody coughed. We were tossed around for eight or ten seconds. Flak helmets were torn off our heads. The ship was filled with flying oxygen bottles, thermos jugs, ear phones, latrine cans, cigarette lighters, cans of fruit juice. We dropped down again with a terrible jolt, and in a few more seconds pulled out into the clear.' "

An official report discussed the morale of the B-29 crews after the blitz got under way: "The phenomenal success of our new tactics had precipitously salvaged the morale and fighting spirit of our crews by providing a degree of battle success proportionate to the effort expended. . . .

"If our crews were encouraged by the low losses and good results of this initial phase, they truly hadn't seen the half of it yet. More and more B-29's were put on the job. Tail guns were reinstalled for minimum protection. Fighter escort was available, if needed. In May and June forces of 400 planes, and more, were launched against the big targets. By 15 June they were so completely destroyed, that the B-29's started a new campaign against more than 60 of the smaller cities. Losses continued to nose dive. In June the average B-29 loss rate per mission was .08%. In July it was .03%. In August it was .02%. In the Marianas, a low altitude incendiary attack on Japan was considered to be about the safest pastime a man could enjoy."

Tokyo became a city of absolute terror. On the night

of April 13th, 327 B-29's again smashed at the capital of Japan, this time striking at the northwest quarter of the city. Each plane carried one 500-pound explosive bomb with its incendiaries, and in the first twenty planes across the target from each of the three attacking waves, the bombs were set to burst in the air—causing the Japanese to abandon fire fighting completely.

The bombs were unnecessary. So terrorized were the Japanese that there would be a repetition of the earlier holocaust that almost everyone in the attack area fled at once. The attack was concentrated against a military-arsenal complex and was not intended as a mass, incendiary raid, but when some of the bombs fell in the urban area near the target sites, the unopposed flames spread unchecked and burned out 11.4 square miles of the city!

Thirty-six hours later the B-29's were taking off from the Marianas for a repeat strike. Two wings smashed the factory-filled city of Kawasaki, just south of Tokyo, while the third wing went after the south Tokyo industrial area. A total of 754 tons of incendiaries ripped the guts out of more than five square miles of the city. The heart of Kawasaki, four square miles, disappeared in flames.

The B-29's hammered again and again at "the city that wouldn't burn," and an avalanche of incendiaries and high explosives poured into Nagoya. Never did that city suffer the wild fury of the fires that seared Tokyo, but so incessant and repeated were the raids that after the fourth mass incendiary strike (plus nine high-explosive bombings) the city of Nagoya was struck from the list of targets. There was nothing left to bomb. The price: 58 bombers and crews.

To the mounting terror of the Japanese, the B-29's were not yet through with Tokyo. Early on the morning of May 24th, the most powerful striking force ever to smash at Japan—520 bombers—poured 3,646 tons of bombs into the south-central urban area.

Within forty-eight hours, while south Tokyo still burned, came the most effective attack of all. A total of 3,252 tons of M-77 bombs, each weighing 500 pounds and combining a tremendous explosive force with the incendiaries, crashed into the heart of Tokyo—into the Ginza commercial area, the government and embassy districts, and the great zone surrounding the Imperial Palace.

When the last bomber left, and the fires of the two attacks had merged, another 22 square miles of the most vital areas of Tokyo were either in ashes or blazing fiercely. The bombing produced the most violent fires ever experienced in Japan. Terrible thermals and towering columns of smoke forced the last waves of B-29's to drop their missiles by radar from a height of 20,000 feet.

This last attack struck Tokyo from the list of targets. The capital had taken seven major incendiary bombings, during which 2,041 of the Superfortresses poured 11,836 tons of incendiaries into the city.

Nearly 57 square miles were totally gutted—more than half of the capital's 111 square miles of area. But it was the most important half, the industrial half, that lay in ruins.

Only a little more than three million people were left in the city. The other millions had fled, abandoning Tokyo to the B-29's.

A tidal wave of fire began to sweep over all of Japan. The great port of Yokohama was struck from the target list after only a single attack. On May 29, 459 Superfortresses unleashed 2,769 tons of bombs and wiped out 85 per cent of the entire metropolitan area.

Osaka, as big as Chicago and second in size only to Tokyo, took a series of smashing raids. After a total of 6,110 tons of bombs crashed into the industrial center, Japanese officials reported that more than 53 per cent of the entire city had been smashed and gutted. More than two million people fled into the countryside.

Kobe took only one more bombing before it was scratched from the list of targets. In a single attack more than three thousand tons of incendiaries wiped out 56 per cent of the city.

The second phase of the incendiary campaign ended in mid-June. Le May had accomplished his primary purpose—the five major industrial cities of Japan were no longer worth bombing. Of the 446 square-mile total in their municipal areas, more than 102 square miles of the most

vital and industrial sections were absolutely destroyed.
Nearly 80 per cent of the industrial potential had either
been smashed, or knocked out of action.

The only major city that had escaped the bombings
was Kyoto, fifth largest Japanese city, and a famed reli-
gious center.

The fire blitz then turned against more than sixty of
the smaller Japanese cities. The results were fantastic as
the B-29's began to tick off target after target, striking as
many as four cities in one day, and completely demolish-
ing their targets.

On June 17th, cities with a population ranging from
100,000 to 350,000 went to the top of the target list. In
thirty days, twenty-three of these cities felt the terrible fire
lash of the Superfortresses.

On July 12th, the campaign began against the final
group of city targets—those with populations of less than
one hundred thousand. The bomb tonnages per attack
soared, reaching a peak on August 2nd, when 855 of the
four-engine raiders poured a hellish concentration of 6,600
tons of bombs onto their selected targets.

The devastation was beyond belief. One night Toyama
was struck as though by a giant meteor. The B-29's circled
the entire city with fire and then sent hurtling into the heart
of the city several thousands of tons of incendiaries.

*In that night the city of Toyama—comparable in size
to Chattanooga—was 97 per cent destroyed.*

By the time the atomic bombs had struck—adding
less than three per cent to the devastated areas—the Superfortresses had gutted a total of 178 square miles in 69
cities. Affected directly was a Japanese population of more
than 21,000,000 people. Cities were being destroyed at the
rate of four at a time, with strikes every two or three days.

The Japanese revealed that *over* 50 per cent of the
area in forty-two cities had been completely burned out.
They listed an additional fifteen cities, including Nagoya
and Osaka, in which, according to A.A.F. estimates, *less*
than 50 per cent was destroyed.

"We had two or three weeks of work left on the cities,
a bit more to do on precision targets, and were just getting

started on transportation," explained General Curtis E. Le May. "Another six months and Japan would have been beaten back into the dark ages—which practically was the case anyhow."

There is another means of judging the effects of the bombings, and it has nothing to do with factories destroyed or how many square miles were burned to the ground.

In six months of fire bombings, starting with the Tokyo raid on the night of March 10th, civilian casualties were more than twice as great as total Japanese military casualties in forty-five months of war.

APPENDIX

In the list of cities that follows an American city is paired with a Japanese city of approximately the same population, to give the reader a more graphic example of the destruction wrought by the B-29 attacks on Japan. No attempt was made to match cities in terms of their industrial importance—only size of population. The per cent of total area destroyed comprises only damage from the B-29 attacks, and does not include damage resulting from the atomic bomb attacks, nor raids by planes of the Fifth and Seventh Air Forces or the Navy.

AMERICAN CITY	JAPANESE COUNTERPART	PER CENT DISASTER
San Diego	Shimonoseki	37.6
Spokane	Moji	23.3
San Antonio	Yawata	21.2
Rochester	Fukuoka	24.1
Nashville	Sasebo	41.4
Waterloo	Saga	44.2
Santa Fe	Omura	33.1
Miami	Omuta	35.9
Grand Rapids	Kumamoto	31.2
Saint Joseph	Oita	28.2
Augusta	Nobeoka	25.2
Richmond	Kagoshima	63.4
Greensboro	Miyakonojo	26.5
Davenport	Miyazaki	26.1
Utica	Ube	20.7

AMERICAN CITY	JAPANESE COUNTERPART	PER CENT DISASTER
no counterpart	Uwajima	54.2
Duluth	Matsuyama	64.0
Sacramento	Kochi	55.2
Butte	Tokuyama	48.3
Toledo	Kure	41.9
Stockton	Imabari	63.9
Macon	Fukuyama	80.9
Knoxville	Takamatsu	67.5
Long Beach	Okayama	68.9
Peoria	Himeji	49.4
Jacksonville	Amagasaki	18.9
Baltimore	Kobe	55.7
Chicago	Osaka	35.1
Fort Worth	Sakai	48.2
Lexington	Akashi	50.2
Salt Lake City	Wakayama	50.0
Cambridge	Nishinomiya	11.9
Ft. Wayne	Tokushima	85.2
Columbus	Uiyamada	41.3
Topeka	Tsu	59.3
Portland	Kawasaki	35.2
Savannah	Chiba	41.0
Battle Creek	Hiratsuka	48.4
Waco	Numazu	42.3
San Jose	Shimizu	42.1
Oklahoma City	Shizuoka	66.1
Wheeling	Chosi	44.2
New York	Tokyo	50.8
Cleveland	Yokohama	57.6
Middletown	Tsuriga	65.1
Evansville	Fukui	86.0
Tucson	Kuwana	75.0
Springfield	Ichinomiya	56.3
Des Moines	Gifu	69.9
Corpus Christi	Ogaki	39.5
Chattanooga	Toyama	98.6
Los Angeles	Nagoya	40.0

AMERICAN CITY	JAPANESE COUNTERPART	PER CENT DISASTER
Charlotte	Yokkaichi	33.6
Lincoln	Okazaki	32.2
Montgomery	Aomori	30.0
Madison	Nagaoka	64.9
Tulsa	Toyohashi	67.9
Hartford	Hammamatsu	60.3
Wilkes-Barre	Maebashi	64.2
Omaha	Sendai	21.9
South Bend	Kofu	78.6
Sioux Falls	Isezaki	56.1
Kenosha	Kumagaya	55.1
Sioux City	Utsunomiya	43.7
Little Rock	Hitachi	72.0
Galveston	Hachioji	65.0
Pontiac	Mito	68.9

Join the Allies on the Road to Victory
BANTAM WAR BOOKS